Unfinished Business

*Putting Your Affairs in Order
with Meaning and Purpose*

COPYRIGHT 2009 BY RON E. DUNN

All rights reserved. No portion of this book may be reproduced, stored in a retrieval system, or transmitted in any form or by any means—electronic, mechanical, photocopy, recording, or other—except for brief quotations in printed reviews, without prior permission from the publisher.

PUBLISHED IN ATLANTA, GEORGIA BY "RON DUNN."
WWW.MYUNFINISHEDBUSINESS.NET

ISBN - 978-1-61623-640-3
Printed in the United States of America
Library of Congress Cataloguing-in-Publication Data

Acknowledgements

I would like to thank the men of IRON and their wives for your initial work and input regarding the forms and variety of information to assemble.

Gayle for challenging me to evolve all of this into book form.

Art, Bruce, Fred, Gayle, Ken, Rachel, Ryan, Tim and Walt for editing and insights.

Pauline for your countless hours of building forms and assembling pilot books.

Rob for creating the web site.

Jeff for cover and layout design.

Dan for your passion, partnership and vision.

My wife, Sandy, for your encouragement and devotion.

This book is dedicated in memory of my grandfather whose love and family leadership lives on.

✯✯✯

"No one wants to have *unfinished business!* Ron does an excellent job in this book helping us avoid unfinished business in the most important areas of our lives. The practical guidance, wisdom and purposeful step-by-step approach are invaluable. Wealthy, poor or in-between, it is important that we leave our families with the information outlined in this book."

Arthur Corbin
President and CEO, Municipal Gas Authority of Georgia

"This is a fine and much needed piece of work. I know that in my life I need to give this closer attention."

Walt Henrichsen
Author and ministry leader

"This book is a fountain of financial and practical wisdom."

Ben Ortlip
President, Kaleo Ranch

"In the world today, whether we are business leaders or not, our main goal is focused on 'finishing well.' Ron Dunn has brought a whole new perspective to what 'finishing well' is all about. He has provided outstanding insights and wisdom that apply to everyone no matter where they find themselves in their walk of life.

"I found *Unfinished Business* to be excellent reading, interesting, biblical, challenging and inspiring. The real life stories added a pertinent dimension that is not often found in instructional books today. I highly recommend that we all incorporate Ron's guidelines found in this book. Thank you for sharing your God-given wisdom. Well done."

Jim Dismore
Chairman/Founder, Kingdom Way Companies

"There is greater wisdom in living proactively than retroactively. Ron Dunn has created a practical resource in *Unfinished Business* that offers specific and hands-on guidance through the process of becoming proactive concerning our earthly affairs. This is a well-crafted tool that will assist many in moving from chaos to clarity."

Dr. Kenneth Boa
Author and President, Reflections Ministries

"Lavonne and I became friends with Ron and Sandy over three decades ago. Through life's various challenges and Ron's rise to national leader in his industry, he continues to methodically advance along a highly organized, well thought out path tempered with good humor and seen though the lens of a deep faith in the Lord. These characteristics provide the framework of *Unfinished Business*. I have studied many books on the topic of financial planning and can't recall one that compares with *Unfinished Business* in the how and why to organize your life. I plan to use it with the clients in my own financial planning practice."

Fred Fernatt
MA, MS, MSFS, CPA/PFS, CFP. ChFC

"I was fortunate to be part of the BETA testing ground for *Unfinished Business*. If you are a 'do-er' and want to get better at pushing through and accomplishing goals; this is a great tool. If you are the head of your household, there are few more important tasks than organizing and documenting your affairs, for your loved ones. I know of no better or timelier guide than *Unfinished Business!* Do it…get it done, and truly 'rest' in God's timeline for your life."

Paul Gouin
President, Wisdom Properties

"This is a great tool and presents an outstanding opportunity to help families. Springing from his practical approach to leadership, Ron Dunn has created an outstanding organizational tool in *Unfinished Business*. I have personally found this life planning exercise to transform my approach to estate planning, financial management and the stewardship of my God given resources. My wife was extremely grateful and secure after I presented her with a completed copy of *Unfinished Business*. We have no promise of tomorrow. 'How do you know what your life will be like tomorrow? Your life is like the morning fog—it's here a little while, then it's gone' (James 4:14, NLT). Let's honestly ask together, is there some unfinished business that needs our immediate attention?"

BOYD BAILEY
CEO, Ministry Ventures and author of
Seeking Daily the Heart of God and *Infusion*

"Some day, sooner than you think, a meeting will be held, probably in your living room, and your favorite chair will sit empty...you will be gone. Will those in attendance say of you, 'He had his house in order'? Every widow will one day turn to her husband's best friend and say, 'Now, what do I do?' Do you want to make the answer to that question as easy as possible?

"Those who plan well live more wisely and leave a stronger legacy. *Unfinished Business* is more than a book, it is a guide and a tool all rolled into one. We all know to do a job well you need the right tools. You now hold in your hands the right tool to help you plan well! Grab a buddy to go through the process with you and get to work...there is a lot at stake."

DAVID H. WILLS
President, National Christian Foundation and author of *Family Money*

Unfinished Business
Putting Your Affairs in Order with Meaning and Purpose

TABLE *of* CONTENTS

FOREWORD:	By Daniel C. Diaddigo	1
CHAPTER 1:	Concerning My Bones WHY GIVE INSTRUCTIONS?	5
CHAPTER 2:	From *Chaos* to *Order* WHERE IS IT?	19
	- Important Documents	27
CHAPTER 3:	From *Order* to *Meaning* WHAT IS OUR FINANCIAL CONDITION?	33
	- Personal Financial Statement	41
	- Assets	43
	- Liabilities	59
	- Current Budget	65
CHAPTER 4:	From *Meaning* to *Knowledge* WHAT DO OTHERS NEED TO KNOW?	67
	- General Information	73
	- Personal Information	75
	- Practical Advice	87

CHAPTER 5: From *Knowledge* to *Wisdom*   105
CONNECTING THE SHIFTING DOTS

- Wise Counsel   113
- Insurance   119
- Social Security   131
- Retirement Income   133
- Disability   141
- Living Will   143
- Estimated Future Budget   145

CHAPTER 6: From *Wisdom* to *Values*   147
PUTTING CLOSURE TO "STUFF"

- Estate Document Checklist   155
  Last Will
  Living Will
  Trusts
  Power of Attorney
  Medical Directive
- Distribution of Possessions   157
- Continued Giving Plan   163
- Funeral Instructions   165

CHAPTER 7: From *Values* to *Hope*   173
GENERATIONAL THINKING!

- Family History   177
- Personal Values   179
- Personal History   183
- Family Tree   187
- Individual Letters   197
- Memo to Family   199
- Closing Summary   201

Foreword

By Daniel C. Diaddigo

Imagine you are alone in an empty stadium, staring at a frozen scoreboard with a game clock that reads *zero*. The men who huddled *with* you have unsnapped their helmets and left the field. The crowd that cheered *for* you has disappeared into the dusk.

You are a touchdown short and the game is over. There's no more time to call an audible. There are no more fans to urge you on, no more teammates to catch your passes. It's just you and the silence where there's supposed to be sound and two words that perch upon your lips unspoken. *"If only...."*

This is the sound of death; it's the sound of unfinished business.

Life... is the *"to be continued"* that extends your story past its final page. Where there is life, there is hope. And, where hope is well-placed—there you will find God.

A while back, Ron came to me with an idea. That Ron had concocted some idea was no surprise. Ron always has ideas. There are two things you should know about Ron. First, you need to know that Ron is an action verb. He's not the sort of guy who tivos life. He lives it.

The second thing you should know is that Ron likes notebooks. In fact, I think that's why I hang out with him. That, and the fact he usually picks up the tab over breakfast. Binder guys are a rare find, I've learned. So, when I happen upon one, I immediately recognize him as a kindred spirit.

On this particular morning, Ron was talking about an organizational binder…over breakfast. So, this was a good morning for me. The binder Ron was discussing was a notebook we had started to develop in our monthly men's group that we call IRON. The notebook contained various forms and was designed to help communicate needed information to our wives and family after our death. At the time, Ron was calling this notebook *Readiness*.

Readiness had traveled past the walls of our IRON group and into the hands of other men who were finding the forms and exercises useful to their planning. Many of these men were giving input and encouraging Ron to turn the forms into a more formal offering.

"They may have a point," he observed. "There seems to be a consistent need to bring some structure to a part of life that typically is full of loose ends. As men, we have generational responsibilities and opportunities. I believe this binder can help guys get organized and take steps to effectively leave what they lived. It's important that we leave behind our hopes and our values, not just a bunch of stuff."

"The thing is…" Ron continued. "We live life full. Most of us are neck deep in responsibilities. Time management is a huge challenge, and, in the midst of all that, we have a hard time wrapping our arms around the reality of what comes next and then applying it to what's happening now. These dots should connect. The one only makes sense in light of the other."

This book is designed to speak to all aspects of our life, not only to our portfolio. Financial advisors can help you transfer wealth to your heirs, but only *you* can communicate your *hope*. Your values and your hope, not your stuff, is what ultimately carries generational impact.

If you're thinking this book is just for old guys, you're wrong. In fact, I'd like a sidebar briefly with the 30 and 40-somethings. I know what you're thinking, because I'm one of you. Most men our age aren't rushing out and to buy books that coach us to put our affairs in order. For one thing, we're not that wise. Most of us are just now figuring out the *good life* doesn't really satisfy. The perks and the promotions didn't exactly live up to their trailers. The big house comes with a mortgage, the big truck with repairs and the big waistline…well, that needs some maintenance as well. We're doing the math and we're waking up to the fact that the junior execs who report to us were in the first grade when we graduated high school. We're wondering if the position and comp plan we fought so hard to achieve has fattened us for a downsize. Our kids are moving into their teens and we are just a few years away from… you have to be kidding… empty-nesters? That's new. Meanwhile, our parents are no longer older, they are old. Each day that passes, we become more acutely aware that the roles are reversing. We are becoming our parents' parents. That's scary. Our senior proms are twenty years in the rearview mirror. Seems like yesterday. Looking through the windshield twenty years and we are… retired? Suddenly, we are questioning the last two decades, wondering if we've been wasting our time. *Deep adulthood* is the road sign we just passed and we haven't yet hit the first exit for a potty break.

We are, at least, asking the right questions now—and with a tinge of urgency. Not much, though. That comes later.

This is the decade we start paying attention to cholesterol and we have our first minor surgery. Our shoulders ache for a whole week after the softball game and our legs feel like they need new shocks. Yes, we are admitting, our bodies are breaking down and we are making adjustments.

To those of us who are paying attention, this decade is mostly about gaining perspective. We want to book the next twenty years toward something that means something; because, we figure, too much from the last twenty years was lost chasing things that don't matter much in the long run. We also determine that we still have enough time to course correct, to right the ship.

This book is about transferring your hope with your wealth, about leveraging the *now* for the *next*. It's about identifying what you have and who you are. It's about planning. It's about communication. It's about cultivating a frame of reference that is other-worldly, one that syncs up the moving parts by helping us to look into our deal from the vantage of another place and through another set of eyes. So, if you bought this book to give to your dad, you might want to read it first. Then grab a buddy or group of guys and go thru it together. It's kind of like working out. It will help to have someone to push you and keep you on task.

Okay. Back to everyone all at once.

Unfinished Business will help you to get your affairs in order before the clock runs out. It will extend your story past your days by helping you pass your hope to your heirs. It will help you discover life even while you prepare for death.

DANIEL C. DIADDIGO

Chapter 1

Concerning my Bones

Why Give Instructions?

Cooperstown, N.Y., is a great place to visit. It is home for The National Baseball Hall of Fame which was founded to preserve history, honor excellence and connect generations. Former ball players, fathers, sons, families and people from all walks of life luxuriate the better part of a day here, soaking in memories, reading about favorite players, and recapturing moments in time. Currently there are 290 inductees. Equally engaging is The Pro Football Hall of Fame, located in Canton, Ohio. Over 200,000 fans of all ages stroll through its aisles each year, closely examining the sculptured busts and reviewing the individual accomplishments of 253 inductees. Their mission statement has been given a plaque of its own: *"To honor, preserve, educate and promote."* Not too far away in Cleveland, Ohio, music enthusiasts enjoy The Rock and Roll Hall of Fame. This museum was built to educate visitors from around the world about the history and significance of rock and roll. The inductees include nearly 250 legendary performers, songwriters and disc jockeys, dating back over 60 years. The entertainment industry put together a very entertaining venue. Displays include a computerized jukebox containing virtually every song of each inductee, etched glass signatures, and three huge screens recounting their careers and music.

God also has a Hall of Fame. You can visit it in Hebrews chapter 11. It honors individuals for the faith they possessed and acted on during a crucial time of their life. This writing preserves history, educates generations on what faith is, demonstrates the significance of faith and encourages men and women to live by faith. There are 17 inductees. Number eight on the list is Joseph. He was the eleventh and second youngest son of Jacob. He was also Jacob's favorite son. His story is amazing.

At age 17, Joseph's father gave him a dazzling, multi-colored coat to wear. He shared dreams which indicated that his older brothers would someday bow before him. They had seen and heard enough, so they faked his death and sold him into slavery. He was bought by Potiphar, one of Egypt's wealthy, and over time, because of his intelligence, values and work ethic; Joseph was promoted to master of the mansion. Great looks and physique were also part of his resume, and they didn't go unnoticed by Potiphar's wife. She tried to seduce him. He refused, stating, "How can I do this great wickedness and sin against God?" She lied about the incident and he landed in prison. After correctly interpreting the dreams of two of Pharaoh's servants, Joseph was forgotten until Pharaoh himself had a few dreams which no one in his court could interpret. Enter Joseph who not only interpreted the dreams, but also laid out a national economic plan in response to the forthcoming world wide famine. Pharaoh immediately promoted him to Vice-Pharaoh, and Joseph successfully led the nation through a great depression that other nations did not see coming. His father and brothers were hit hard as crops dried up and cattle died. Eventually 10 of his brothers traveled to Egypt, bowed before Joseph and pleaded for food, clueless that they were kneeling before the very brother whose dreams they rejected.

The full story can be found in Genesis 37 – 50. You can read of Joseph's induction into the Hall of Fame in Hebrews 11:22. But, before checking it out, take one guess as to why Joseph made the cut. What did he do that demonstrated his faith in such a way that he joins the other sixteen inductees in God's "Hall of Fame"? Was it because he rejected the seduction of a powerful woman? Nope. Guess again. Was it because he remained faithful while living in prison all those years, knowing he was betrayed by his brothers, sold into slavery, falsely convicted by his owner, and then forgotten by a person of influence who he had helped? Wrong again. Let's read it. The answer surprised me.

Hebrews 11:22: *"By faith Joseph, when he was dying, made mention of the departure of the children of Israel and gave instructions concerning his bones."*

Joseph is in God's Hall of Fame because he gave funeral instructions! The actual event is recorded in Genesis 50:25. Joseph could have been enshrined in a pyramid, mummified with the Pharaohs. He could have solidified his place of recognition in world history. He could have bestowed great historical honor on himself for what he accomplished during this time in Egypt. He took a pass. He held fast to the promise that God would someday lead the Israelites to a Promised Land and that was the place to which he wanted his bones carried and buried. At his death Joseph clearly communicated his faith and his hope, and gave instructions accordingly. God made a promise. Joseph believed Him. He identified himself with God's promise.

Throughout this book we will be discussing and filling out numerous forms covering a variety of aspects relating to putting our affairs in order. It will require some goal setting and planning. It will also provide framework for communicating your values and your hope and then like Joseph, you can give instructions accordingly.

CHAPTER 1 : *Concerning* my *Bones*

The Passport Project

Every day in America, 6,815 die. Included are loving husbands, fathers, wives, and mothers who die without properly organizing their affairs, leaving their loved ones to bear these burdens on top of the tremendous grief. *Unfinished Business* is an initiative to help change that. We've gathered all the important items into an easy to follow process.

One out of one people die. We all know we're going on this trip. The last thing we want to do is fail to file the necessary documents. As we prepare for this inevitable journey, the first thing we'll need is a Passport. A passport certifies citizenship, entitles protection, validates identity and allows passage. Jesus Christ provides that to us through his life, death and resurrection. He has done His part. Our part is to place our faith in Him, reflected by a life of obedience.

I was given several suggestions for the title of this book. "The Passport Project" was one of the leading candidates because of the multiple analogies and word pictures that apply to properly planning an over seas vacation and preparing for our passage into eternal life. Prior to that unknown day when our "Passport" will be checked, it is both wise and will be greatly appreciated to give instructions "concerning our bones." This book is a step by step guide to help us get our house in order before that final trip ahead.

Goal Setting

I've always liked setting goals.

When I was 30 I developed a list of 40 things I would like to do before the age of 40. Attend the seventh game of a World Series, secure tickets to a Super Bowl involving the Green Bay Packers, look over the Grand Canyon with my wife, travel to Hawaii with my family, golf Pebble Beach, run up the "Rocky" stairs in Philadelphia, avoid buying slacks with greater than a 35" waist, read one book a month, read through the entire Bible. Thirty-eight of these goals were realized and at age 40, I reloaded with 50 more. Today my list consists of 60.

I really can't remember a time when organizing events and setting goals wasn't a part of my thinking. Whether it was the number of As on my report card, how quickly I could finish my paper route, how many times out of 100 I could flip heads with a baseball card, being the first in the car to call out 100 "spuds" (Volkswagen beetles) on family road trips or the consecutive string of free throws in the backyard; most activities involved goals. I guess it is no surprise that I launched a career in sales and business management.

Proper goal setting usually produces favorable results.

(7)

At the very least, goal setting helps us review what is in front of us, prioritize what is important, project what seems possible and establish a targeted result for specific efforts.

Planning

So, is this a self-help book that establishes proper goal setting as the catalyst for putting our affairs in order? No, not hardly. It is more a book about planning. There is an important difference between planning and goal setting. Goal setting involves what I will do if not thwarted by Providence. Planning involves what I will do in response to Providence. Providence is the control exercised by God.

Action leads to an outcome, but the past two decades and my grey hair have taught me that outcome is not totally predictable. My goal is to live three more decades and be actively involved with family and friends throughout these years. Providence may lead differently. Suppose I am told by a doctor that I have only a short time to live. How would this scenario affect my view of life, my goals, my planning, the manner in which I invest my remaining time? I suggest that the degree to which this would alter my current perspective and daily activities is the distance between my current view of what is important in life and God's view of what is important in life.

Like Moses and the nation of Israel in the Exodus, we cannot predict the future. When the "cloud" moves, we must act on instinct and demand, despite what our goals prescribed. No one can deny that our life here is short and often unpredictable. This is Providence and, in response, we should make provisions.

This book is about organization and planning. It is about putting our affairs in order with meaning and purpose. When organization is applied to proper planning, the result is meaningful activity.

Until recently I, like most, had not properly applied planning to the handing over of my affairs. I had fun setting goals for things that may or may not happen, but neglected planning for what will happen. Planning properly, by putting my affairs in order, never reached a position of high priority. I walked around it for a reason. It seemed very complicated. It seemed a distant need. I really didn't want to think much about it. I didn't know how to go about it. Yes, it definitely seemed confusing. I knew the ball of yarn stood in front of me, like the proverbial elephant in the room, but untangling it meant lawyers, accountants, insurance review, estate planning, tax projection and an even longer list of similar things I wasn't even thinking about. It was pretty easy to come up with something else to do, every time it came to mind. I would read things like Moses' words and insights on the shortness of life in Psalm 90, but then quickly shrug them off.

That changed a couple of years ago.

How Do You Prepare for Something like This?

John died at a fairly young age. I had not experienced the loss of a close friend since high school. As I was sitting in our packed church, thinking back on conversations I had with him, my thoughts went to his family. I wondered how they were coping. I couldn't imagine. How do you prepare for something like this? John died leaving behind a wife, two sons, two daughters and a son-in-law. They sat in a row diagonal to my left, eyes fixed between tears upon the podium. I watched as one man, then another, then another and still another stepped to the platform and celebrated John's life, recalling his heart, discussing his character and sharing his hope. They told stories that represented a deep and inspiring level of intimacy. John's death brought sadness, but his story and all that surrounded him was inspiring.

I sat in silence with tears running down my cheeks, convicted and still with my thoughts.

This is right.

This is God's design for our lives.

This is the love Jesus spoke of.

People involved with other people.

Sharing life and investing time together.

Consistently.

Supporting.

Caring.

Encouraging each other.

Making a difference.

When the service ended I approached Jim, one of the men who had stepped up to the podium and complimented him and the group for their role and all they had done. He explained to me that they had all known each other for nearly 13 years and were in a men's group together. Through those years they had experienced life together and in the last year they prepared for death together. I asked him how Robin and their family were going to be monetarily. He said John had put his affairs in order.

The Elephant in the Room

During the months that followed my radar was suddenly alerted to comments and questions consistently emerging from Sandy, my wife.

Where would she find information about certain things if I was not around?

We received a letter from the IRS asking for some back-up information. I went to my office, opened a file drawer, pulled out what was requested and handed it to my wife to copy and send. She looked at me and said, "You know, if you weren't here, I wouldn't have known where to find that."

If I was not here, she would not have known where to find that.

Wait a minute! If I was not here? OK, I had recently celebrated my 50th birthday, but. But what? The bottom line is something could happen to any of us suddenly and as it was, our affairs were scattered, scrambled, incomplete and in many areas unaddressed.

It became clear to me that it was time to address the elephant in the room. It was time to apply proper planning. It was time to talk about things we would rather not talk about. It was time to organize all of our affairs. It was time to prepare for crisis. It was time to prepare for the inevitable. It was time to be a steward in this area. It was time to think generationally. It was time to think practically and then document values and hope beyond what I leave behind. It was time to tackle the temporal in light of the eternal.

Proverbs 27:17 states: *"As iron sharpens iron, so a man sharpens the countenance of his friend."*

IRON. That's the name of our men's group. Eight of us meet together once a month for six hours. The goal is to grow old together, providing iron to each other in all areas of life based on truth from God's Word.

I presented to the men in IRON this project of setting our affairs in order and suggested we take it on together. Everyone acknowledged the need and agreed to move forward. After discussing the objectives, we decided the first thing to do was interview our wives, to gain their perspective. The goal was to identify areas of concern that *they* had, which we might not think of. The questions we asked included:

- If I was gone, what would you not know that you wish I had explained?
- What type of information would you want to have readily available?
- What could I get ready now that would help you get through?
- What would you wish I had included in a filing system for easy reference?

As suspected, much of what they answered included items that we would never have come up with on our own. This became a work in progress that spread over nine months. Many of the line items on the forms included in this book are a result of each couple's input.

You Don't Want to Prepare for a Crisis When You Are in the Crisis

I attend a monthly meeting of CEOs. I gave a copy of the original workbook (which we called "Readiness") to each of the business men attending. This served two purposes. Each of the men admitted that they had unfinished business in this area, so it was a very practical exercise for them. Plus, they provided great insights to help improve what we were putting together. Keith had just lost his younger brother. As he was working his way through each section, Keith's comment was: *"You don't want to prepare for a crisis when you are in the crisis."* During his brother's year-long health battle, he faced myriad emotions ranging from denial to depression to hope. There was so much to deal with physically, emotionally and spiritually. As a result, he never was able to completely put his affairs in order.

A few days after I sent out a rough copy of *Unfinished Business* to several friends and mentors for their input, I received the following e-mail from the general manager of our golf club:

> *Dear Member,*
> *It is with a sad heart that I inform you that Tom Mudry passed away on December 29. Mr. Mudry experienced a strong but brief 4-week battle with esophagal cancer. Mr. Mudry was an active White Columns member, and he will be greatly missed by all.*

Below is an excerpt from the obituary in the Atlanta Journal-Constitution:

> MUDRY – Mr. Thomas A. Mudry, age 50, of Alpharetta, GA, died December 29, 2008 after a brief battle with cancer. Mr. Mudry, an avid golfer and outdoorsman, especially enjoyed spending time with family and friends and was loved by everyone who knew him. He was employed for 28 years with General Motors Corporation, where he held various Executive positions in the Financial, Dealer Network, Sales, Service and Marketing Departments. Survivors include his loving wife and precious children age 10 and age 7.

Sandy and I had just left for Disneyland with our son, his wife and our two grandsons. I read the email in our hotel room. When I shared the message with my son, his reaction was very much the same as mine:

- Shock: We just saw Tom, and he had seemed perfectly fine.

- Disbelief: With shaking heads, we did not want to accept the message.

- Memories: Tournaments we played in. Stories he told. His passion. His career. His wife. His children. Our last conversation.

- What if this happened to me? Are my affairs in order?

Four weeks!

On Thanksgiving Day he seemed fine. Before New Years he had died.

Four weeks!

Amidst the physical and emotional battle, there is so much I would want to say and so much I would want to leave with those who are closest to me. Keith was right; you don't want to prepare for a crisis when you are in the crisis. There is sound wisdom in putting our affairs in order while we are in good mental, physical and emotional health.

To help organize this effort, we have prepared 70 forms over seven chapters.

Book Layout

Unfinished Business is laid out in seven chapters.

Chapter 1
- Interview your spouse, or those closest to you utilizing the four questions provided at the end of this chapter. This will help identify some of the personal information they would like to have readily available when you are no longer here..

Chapter 2
- Establish an Organized System for putting your affairs in order.

- Set up a specific file cabinet or filing tub to house all of the needed documents.

- Create an empty file folder clearly labeled and identified for each of the items on the Location of Important Documents worksheets.

UNFINISHED BUSINESS

CHAPTER 3
- Complete an updated Personal Financial Statement.
- List all Key Assets
- Document a Current Estimated Budget.

CHAPTER 4
- Provide important General Information
- Safety Deposit Boxes, Computer Instructions and Hidden Items
- Household Mechanics and Maintenance
- Practical Decisions and Advisors

CHAPTER 5
- Life Decisions and Wise Counsel
- Insurance Overview
- Retirement benefits
- Projected Future Income
- Estimated Future Budget
- Disability
- Living Will
- Estimated Future Budget

CHAPTER 6
- Last Will
- Living Trust
- Insurance Trust
- Charitable Trust
- Power of Attorney
- Distribution of Possessions

(14)

- Continued-Giving Plan

- Funeral Instructions and Special Requests

CHAPTER 7
- Family History

- Personal Values

- Personal History

- Family Tree, Memories and Traditions

- Thoughts and Advice

- Memo to Your Family

- Closing Summary

Finishing Unfinished Business

Chances are that without much effort you will quickly be able to come up with numerous ways to leave this book and countless reasons to procrastinate and not bring to completion certain of the sections for putting your affairs in order. While this was still in its initial rough form, over 70% of the forty men who asked to use it did not finish all of the sections. Most of the unfinished sections involved the areas where outside professional help was needed, such as setting up a will, establishing a trust and bringing insurance needs up to date. Some involved letter writing, family history, and personal values. The 30% who finished the project had established deadlines and an accountability partner for completion.

Following are some suggestions to help you avoid procrastination and to successfully cross the finish line of putting your affairs in order:

TOTALLY COMPLETE ONE CHAPTER EVERY TWO WEEKS
Establish a specific goal and time frame for completion. The book has been set up in seven chapters with corresponding work-sheet sections. Depending on your time demands, one chapter every week might be overly aggressive. If you pre-establish blocks of time, one chapter every two weeks should allow for adequate quality completion.

ACCOUNTABILITY
Make yourself accountable to someone for finishing each section on time. Doing this with others can prove to be very helpful both for accountability and for the sharing of ideas. Including

your spouse as an accountability person would probably provide the best partnership for finishing all sections.

Men's Groups
If you are going through this book with a men's group that meets every week; the recommended schedule would be to allow two weeks for each chapter. Week one involves reading and discussing the contents of the chapter and reviewing the affiliated forms. Week two involves further discussing the applications of the content, updating each person's progress and addressing any questions that may have come up. If the group meets every other week, establish a goal for everyone to accomplish one chapter per meeting. If you meet once a month for an extended period of time; assign two chapters per session.

Pre-plan Time and Resources
Look ahead to Chapters 5 and 6 and pre-schedule time to address some of the larger items. These include establishing a will, a living will, a power of attorney and trusts.

Set Up Files.
Take out some time on the front-end to organize your filing cabinet for housing all of the documents listed in Chapter 2. This will provide an organizational foundation that will prove helpful, as you work your way through each section.

Personalize This Work
Think outside the box. This book provides a framework, but is not all inclusive. Your files and finished project should be personalized to your life and desires.

Network
Be interactive during the process. Involve your spouse and kids. Whether you are tackling this project alone or with a group, share ideas and get input from others who are facing the same decision-making challenges.

Professional Help
Properly, correctly, thoroughly and legally setting up your affairs will require professional input and help. We highly recommend that you see legal counsel and involve the help of a professional accountant when finalizing the items discussed in this book and particularly Chapters 5 and 6. This will help assure compliance.

Disclaimer
The information shared in this book is not intended to replace or provide legal advice. This is a gathering or practical information that will help those who use it gather together much of the information that will greatly assist loved ones in settling their estate. It is also intended to help those who use it think beyond the stuff we leave.

As you get into this, if you come across something that is extremely helpful or if there is something you would like input on, visit our website: www.myunfinishedbusiness.net. This site will serve as both a resource and an avenue by which you can provide input.

Point of Reference

The forms, documents and organizational framework that Unfinished Business provides have multiple applications. I believe that The Bible is God's Word and contains the ultimate source of truth. This book is written from a Christian perspective with the primary audience intended to be those desiring to put their affairs in order with meaning and purpose.

We hope that everyone who uses it finds it to be a helpful framework for organizing material things, in light of eternal hope.

Work in Progress

Unfinished Business has been tested, but is not perfected. It is a work-in-progress. It is intended that each user adds to, and personalizes, the forms and documents..

We encourage you to log in and register at www.myunfinishedbusiness.net. This site will be regularly updated with helpful information. We look forward to hearing from you.

Assignment for Chapter 1

Before getting started with the forms provided (beginning in Chapter 2) we encourage you to utilize the same four questions used by IRON and interview your spouse. Keep the answers at hand and reference them as you complete each chapter. If there is anything on your list that is not covered in the book, personalize your files by adding this information and please share your additions with us by logging into the web site listed.

The questions to ask include:

- If I was gone what would you not know, that you wish I had explained?

- What type of information would you want to have readily available?

- What could I get ready now, that would help you get through?

- What would you wish I had included in a filing system for easy reference?

CHAPTER 2

From *Chaos* to *Order*

WHERE IS IT?

Location of Important Documents and Information

Life lists are becoming more and more popular as people seek meaningful ways to spend their time, energy and money. Aspiring artists, first time sky-divers and world travelers are increasingly putting their life goals down on paper—and on the Internet. These "bucket list" creations include 100 things to do before you die, 50 foods to eat, 1001 books you must read, 28 places to see, 1000 recordings to hear, 12 things to photograph, 20 hamburgers to eat, 13 places to dine and 100 geeky things for non-geeks to experience.

In a round-about way, this is what we will be working on through the seven chapters of this book. Only instead of focusing on things we would like to experience, we will be identifying and putting in order what we would like to leave behind for others, and we'll be discussing how to leave it. We begin not with a "bucket list," but with a file list.

Getting Started

I enjoy playing golf with my son, Ryan. When he birdies hole #1 and I don't, he'll put his arm over my shoulder as we walk off the green and say, "You can't win them all unless you win the first hole." My response: "It's not how you start, it's how you finish!"

(19)

Sometimes how we start does have a lot to do with how well we finish. This is one of those times. In the weeks ahead you will be utilizing various forms to help put your affairs in order.

It is important to start by establishing an organized system which allows for easy reference and retrieval. If you don't take the time to establish this infrastructure on the front end, you will find yourself shuffling papers, duplicating efforts and struggling to bring simplicity and orderliness to your affairs. Step one is to establish clearly marked individual files to house each of the key documents listed on the Location of Important Documents overview sheet, which you will find at the end of this chapter. As part of the initial steps, designate a filing cabinet or box to organize all these in one safe and easy-to-reference place.

Kill the Clutter Bug

Have you ever noticed how clutter distracts and pulls energy? When I allow my in-box to overflow and I start piling things on my desk or around my office; the disorganization starts screaming at me, distracting from priorities, destroying clear focus and reducing my productivity. At times like this I have to stop, get organized and move from chaos to order. This does not come naturally, in most endeavors. It takes time, planning, vision, strategy and discipline. When order is introduced to disorganization, everything moves at a smoother pace.

We have a practice in our office called "Road Trip." It has been proven that clutter at best doubles the amount of energy and time it takes to accomplish an objective. Clutter puts at risk the accomplishment of any objective. Because of this dynamic, we "police" the clutter in our offices and workspaces and when it becomes obvious that chaos has set in, we interrupt our Monday morning staff meeting and go on a 'road trip" to the infected area and put a deadline on bringing order back into that area. When I announce that its time for a road trip, the response is usually: "oh-no." No one likes to have their disorganization exposed. My daughter, Rachel, serves the function of providing organization in the office where she works. She coordinates the agenda and flow for the large variety of outside visitors and oversees supplies for the 300-plus employees. They honored her this year on her birthday with "you're the bomb" and "who's your momma?" banners. One of the office managers commented that Superman wears Rachel pajamas. This is the impact that effective organization can bring to any endeavor. That is our goal as we work toward putting our affairs in order.

Do not short-cut Step 1. Take the needed time to establish an organized retrieval system. Set up your files. Move from chaos to order, in the gathering of key information. Order is important, both now and in the future. Someday those closest to you will be swimming in the chaos created by your departure. One of the best initiatives you can undertake for them is the development of an orderly system for your affairs....

Mediocre, Average, Ordinary, Good Enough

None of these adjectives portray a positive image, yet that is the effort sometimes given to the endeavors we pursue. If you follow the template provided, and complete all of the forms in each of the chapters in this book, you will be farther ahead than 99% of the population; your affairs will be better organized today and your loved ones will be better prepared when you are no longer here. That is good. But, it may not be good enough.

What do I mean?

Multiple books have been written and numerous seminars conducted on the dynamic in our culture of "good" being the lethal enemy of "best." I witnessed this multiple times while heading up a national sales force. I can think of countless people who had incredible potential, but settled for less than their best because it seemed good enough to get by. There is a vast difference between going through the motions to accomplish a task and purposefully working to achieve great results. These dynamics and principles apply to most experiences in life. They certainly apply to *Unfinished Business*.

If you rush through the reading, and you approach this as a task, that frame of mind cannot help but result in just enough effort to get by, to fill in forms and to get a whole lot of facts assembled. If, however, you start with the desire to put your affairs in order in a manner that is reflective of you, your work, values and hope; if you take ownership and set your own goals for what these files will reflect and keep before you specific people and the specific results YOU desire to accomplish; then by the end of Chapter 7 you will have assembled a finished product of tremendous generational value. All we have done with this book is ask pertinent questions, share applicable thoughts and provide appropriate forms. You must apply, expand and personalize it to reflect your heart's desire.

This will require long-term thinking. This will necessitate that you keep in mind each of the people for whom you are preparing each file. You must switch gears a little and see beyond these times to a possible time of crisis or a natural end when this work will be greatly needed. This perspective will push you to explore, learn, expand your current level of understanding and then move forward. It will squelch procrastination. It will inspire you to enter new and unknown areas with a passion to gain new understanding and to bring application.

I encourage you to give this your best effort.

Personalize it.

Make it your own.

Establish this as a reflection of the life you have lived, the values you have embraced, the desires you carry in your heart and the hope that endures within you.

Why is it important to take inventory of your key documents?

Recently my wife and I visited a cemetery to review burial options. I asked Angela, the lady giving us the "tour," what the most difficult part of her job is. She didn't hesitate to respond as she described the dynamics of when someone dies without having their affairs in order. Loved ones are left with the disheartening task of trying to bring order to affairs during a time of grieving. Angela described countless examples of family members whose grieving turns to anger as they battle through the tangled mess of disorganized, unfinished business left behind.

Establishing files and keeping inventory will

1. help bring order to your affairs;

2. assure that pieces are not left undone; and,

3. provide clarity and organization to the proper settling of affairs after we are gone.

Keeping this in one easy-to-review place will help in both the preparation and the administration.

What do these documents represent?

We live in a complicated world. Taxes, laws, legal standards, living wills, security codes….. how did we get here? That could be a book unto itself. The bottom line is there are a whole lot of fences built for our protection. Our part is to first understand the restrictions and opportunities; secondly, make sure we comply; and thirdly, make it easy for our loved ones to access everything, once we are gone.

These documents include all of the account numbers, codes, pin numbers, legal language, explanations, instructions, titles, agreements, obligations, settlements, tax information, trusts, will and wishes associated with your life and what you are leaving behind.

How did we come up with this list?

This list of needed documents was compiled from input received from a variety of people. In addition to interviewing our wives, we consulted with a legal firm, an investment broker, an insurance consultant and an accountant. We also spoke with several families who have experienced death and all of the hassles and legal ramifications associated with the death of a loved one.

Why put our affairs in order? What are the benefits?

Disorder can be our worst enemy. Human nature is not at ease with disorder. We are instructed in I Corinthians 14:40 to "let all things be done decently and in order."

Good order provides foundation. It is reflective of God. The fact is we need to place things in their proper order. When we do, we are following a pattern that God gave us. He knows because He created us in His image. Life functions best when it is orderly. Orderliness by definition is not random. Orderliness provides a pattern that we can walk in.

"Putting our house in order" relates to everything our life touches; all of our things, but also our values and our hope. While putting things in order takes a little bit of time and attention, it is far less difficult and time-consuming than living with and leaving disorder.

What impact will this orderliness have upon your spouse and your family?

Dealing with death is one of the most difficult things we all face, this side of eternity. Life, as we knew it, changes. Many things end. Routines change. Responsibilities change. It is common in marriages and family for each person to take on specific roles and take care of specific responsibilities. *Unfinished Business* is designed to reach into many of those areas, and help to provide a bridge and smoother transition.

How often should I refresh these documents?

An annual review is recommended. Tax time provides a natural framework to update files and adjust documents, as needed.

No Small Feat

This project that you have decided to tackle is not an easy one. It will take time. It will take effort. It will require attention, follow-up, commitment.

Avoid rushing.

Be still.

Think things through.

Pray.

Get input.

Keep those for whom you are preparing this book clearly in mind as you work your way through each section.

Your File List: Where is it?

FORMS 1 – 2

This first exercise, in and of itself, is really quite simple. However, do not allow that to minimize its importance and do not allow yourself to fall behind in organizing your affairs. Proceed with purpose. Follow a three-step approach.

1. Begin by establishing a filing cabinet or filing tub to house all of the forms and documents. A fireproof unit would be ideal.

2. Next clearly label individual files for each of the items listed on Forms 1, 2A and 2B.

3. Hang these folders within your filing unit.

This will provide you with the proper framework for moving forward without confusion, duplication of efforts or disorganization.

The documents listed on Forms 2A and 2B entitled Location of Important Documents will be dealt with in future chapters. Those items listed on Form 1 should be located and filed now.

The primary goals in this section are to

1. Establish an organizational system and location for housing important documents

2. Place the proper documents in these files.

This first form titled: "Location of Important Documents" consolidates our loose ends to a list. The file system will provide framework for the remaining forms and will help bring order to the chaos of scattered and disconnected pieces.

Electronic Filing

On the back cover of this book you will find a personal identification number. If you log on to the internet and go to WWW.MYUNFINISHEDBUSINESS.NET you will be able to access all of the forms online. Click on the tab for Electronic Forms. When prompted, insert your ID number and follow the instructions. You will be able to download and print all of the forms to hard copy and download free software tools for encryption so that your electronic files are private and secure. There are multiple advantages of being able to access and work with this information in this manner. We recommend that you scan and store as much as possible, together in a secure electronic file. Backing up this information by storing it on an external hard drive or using an online backup service is advisable, but do not neglect bringing order to all of this in hard copy as well by placing originals in the filing system we are discussing. This will allow for easy access and review by your loved ones after you are gone. We also recommend that you place your documents or external hard drives in a fireproof safe or bank lockbox to protect yourself from fire or water damage and theft.

Get Started

STEP 1:
Resolve to give this your best effort.

STEP 2:
Set up your files. Begin by establishing an empty file for each item. Use the "Location of Important Documents" forms as a template for the files you will need. It will be very helpful if you keep a copy of all the working files together in one filing drawer or fire-proof file box as you move forward through this project.

STEP 3:
Take time to personalize the document list. Refer back to the list you compiled at the end of Chapter 1. Identify additional documents needed that are specific to your personal situation and add them to your list.

STEP 4:
Establish two locations for copies of these documents. One place for originals and one place for copies of the originals.

STEP 5:
Beware of identity theft. This is a growing problem. The information in these files could be very problematic if it got into the wrong hands. Please review the WARNING we have included in the final page of this book and be very careful concerning whom you share this information with, including the location of your documents.

STEP 6:
Plan ahead. Some of these documents will require professional involvement for completion. As you review the documents currently incomplete, establish goals for yourself and make appropriate

appointments. Be very deliberate and attentive in these areas. Avoid procrastination and bring each document to completion.

STEP 7:
Establish deadline dates for the completion of each file.

STEP 8:
Get started and enjoy the process.

Location of Important Documents

FORM 1

(Each of these documents are self-standing and do not have a coordinating form in this book)

Updated: _____

Document	Location of Original	Location of Copy
PERSONAL DOCUMENTS		
Birth Certificates:		
Marriage Certificate:		
Social Security Card:		
Passport:		
Other:		
PERSONAL ACCOUNTS		
Company Pension:		
IRA:		
401k:		
Section 529 Education Plan:		
Other:		
PERSONAL AGREEMENTS		
Business:		
Pre-Nuptial:		
Post-Nuptial:		
Other:		
TAX FILINGS		
Income Taxes:		
Property Taxes:		
DEEDS		
Cemetery:		
Other:		
LEASES		
Buildings:		
Automobiles:		
Other:		
MISCELLANEOUS PAPERS		
Children Adoption Papers:		
Citizenship Papers:		
Divorce Decree Settlement:		
Military Discharge (DD214):		
Other:		
CONTRACTS		
Employment:		
Independent Contractors:		
Other:		

Location of Important Documents

Form 2a (Pg. 1 of 2)

(Each of these documents has a coordinating form in this book)

Updated: _____

Form	Form Number	Location of Original	Location of Copy
Personal Financial Statement:	3		
Real Estate:	4		
Automobiles and Other Vehicles:	5		
Valuable Personal Property:	6		
Stocks You Hold:	7		
Bonds You Hold:	8		
Other Investments:	9		
Receivables:	10		
Additional Key Assets:	11		
Debt Details:	12		
Credit Cards:	13		
Bank Accounts:	14		
Current Estimated Budget:	15		
General Information:	16		
Safe-Deposit Box Inventory:	17-18		
Home Safe/File Cabinet Inventory:	19		
Items Loaned to Others:	20		
Computer Instructions:	21		
Hidden Items of Value:	22		
Help Household Answers:	23		
Household Mechanics Overview:	24		
Household Appliance:	25		
Neighborhood Directory:	26		
Automotive Strategy:	27		
Purchasing Decisions:	28		
Key Advisors:	29-34		
Insurance Inventory:	36-40		
Social Security:	41		
Company Retirement Benefits:	42		
Estimate of Retirement Income:	43		
Future Income upon Loss of Spouse:	44		
Inheritance Information:	45		
In the Event of My Incapacity:	46		
Estimated Future Budget:	48		

(29)

Location of Important Documents
(Each of these documents has a coordinating form in this book)

Form 2b (Pg. 2 of 2)

Updated: _____

Form	Form Number	Location of Original	Location of Copy
Estate Documents Checklist: (each of these should have their own file)	49		
Will:			
Living Will:			
Living Trust:			
Insurance Trust:			
Charitable Trust:			
Minor's Trust:			
General Power of Attorney:			
Medical Power of Attorney:			
Medical Directive:			
Distribution of Possessions:	50-52		
Continued Giving Plan:	53		
Funeral Instructions/Who to Notify:	54-55		
Funeral Special Requests:	56-57		
Family History:	58		
Personal Values:	59-60		
Personal History:	61-62		
Family Tree:	63-64		
Letters to Individuals:	68		
Memo to My Family:	69		

(31)

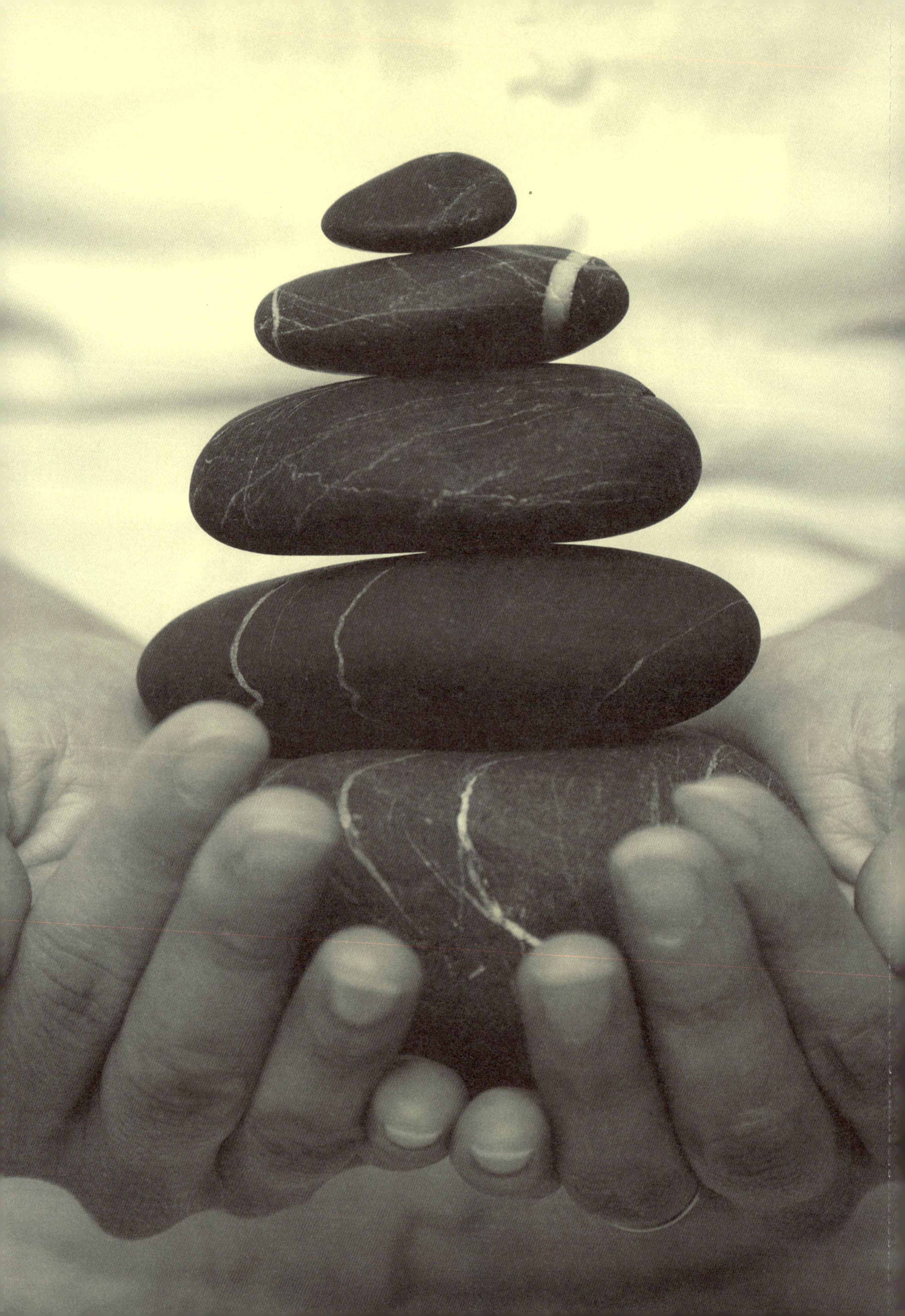

CHAPTER 3

From *Order* to *Meaning*

What Is Your Financial Condition?

"So teach us to number our days that we may apply our hearts unto wisdom."
PSALM 90:12

What Are Your Assets and Liabilities?
What is Your Current Budget?

My partner and I founded our company 12 years ago. While sitting in the lobby of the Ritz Carlton in downtown Atlanta explaining our business plan to a potential investor, he looked me in the eyes and said: "Someday you and Jon are going to be wealthy men." I recently called my prophetic friend and told him that two years ago we might have given some credence to his prediction, but given the current economic challenges, I needed to let him know that we don't think he had a clue what he was talking about. Without hesitation he responded: "My projections have a 10-year warranty." We had a good laugh and then went on to talk about current business conditions, economic cycles, and historical numbers. He has a tremendous advantage when it comes to some of this. If you call his Chicago-based business, you will hear a recording that states, "established in 1874." They have a multi-generational business dating back over 135 years. He refers to a financial statement as a temporal scoreboard.

Establishing a Scoreboard

What a great perspective to have. Rather than thinking only about this season or this year or these three years or even this decade, they can lay out literally one hundred years of historical data to bring order, balance and meaning. What is applicable in business is often applicable in our personal lives. In this chapter we will be talking about the value of establishing a Personal Financial Statement. This is an important step in moving from chaos to order, and from order to meaning. Your personal financial statement can serve as a scoreboard that will help identify your financial condition today, provide historical progress over time and thereby assist in making strategic decisions. A Personal Financial Statement will help you number and numbering is the means by which we bring order to things.

How Do You Ascribe Meaning?

It has been said that the first job of any religion is to help us define purpose. Why are we here? As you take inventory of your life and reflect on what you have and what you do; what process do you use to ascribe meaning? When you factor in the existence and presence of God, does anything change? Does God's existence help define your purpose?

It is my observation that a whole lot of people get caught up thinking that God wants to take their money. The truth is God doesn't want your money to take you. If there is one thing regarding our finances that God desires, it is that we honor Him with what we have. All of Scripture asserts that this life is the seedtime of eternity. The primary purpose for living this life is not to bring glory to ourselves. The primary purpose for this life is to honor God and prepare for an eternity with Him.

However long we live, our days will seem few. An expression that I have heard through-out life is how swiftly the years fly by. The first time I remember my mother elaborating on this statement was on my parents' 25th wedding anniversary. That was over 30 years ago. This year they will celebrate their 58th Anniversary. We are no longer talking about years. Decades move quickly. Moses states that one thousand years in God's sight is like a day. What are we to take from this? How does this affect our thinking, our planning and our activities? How should we invest the time we have?

These are big questions. Your answers will reveal your relationship with things, people and God. At the heart of this discussion stands what is most important to you, that one thing that takes center stage. It could be you. It could be another person. It could be things and possessions. It should be your relationship with God. In that center is God's desire that we love others, live a life of obedience and bring thanksgiving and glory to Him.

As we fill our days using the gifts He has given us, we will grow assets. Our responsibility then is to steward those assets in light of the time we are given. The world system says the more you have and the bigger the number on the temporal scoreboard, the better off you are. God's economy says the more you have the more accountable you are for what is on the scoreboard. It is easy to understand the values of the world. Apart from eternal accountability, the person with the biggest pile wins. In Luke 12:48, however, Jesus explains that to whom much is given, of him much will be required.

It is not wise to be frivolous with our assets from a temporal or an eternal standpoint. Our planning reflects our priorities. In this chapter, we will spend time developing an up- to-date personal financial statement, listing financial assets and liabilities, and then applying all of this to a current monthly budget.

Personal Financial Statement

In Psalm 90, Moses asked God to help him number his days. Just as our days define the boundaries of our total time on earth; the personal financial statement and budget statement establish the boundaries of our resources. Numbering our days gives us a framework for planning. By numbering our days we can make wiser choices regarding how we utilize our time. In a similar fashion, a Personal Financial Statement helps number our financial resources and gives framework for both planning and decisions relating to how we utilize our wealth.

Developing and maintaining a Personal Financial Statement serves a number of purposes. It provides an effective snapshot of your personal financial condition and through the years will provide a comparative scorecard. It also enables you to quickly examine the connectedness of your holdings. Questions you will want to ask include: What is the ratio of your assets to liability? Is my financial condition tracking in the right direction each year? For example, you will list your home as an asset. In the liabilities column, you would note any corresponding mortgages. As you consider taking out a loan for remodeling, adding a swimming pool or landscaping, you will want to properly estimate what the increase in appraised value will be in the asset column verses the increase in liability through an additional loan. The impact of the new loan payment must then be analyzed in your current budget, which is also covered in this chapter.

As you fill out your Personal Financial Statement (PFS) keep in mind that ASSETS are any item of economic value that you own, especially that which could be converted to cash. Examples are: cash, securities, real estate, a car, jewelry, furniture and other property. LIABILITIES represent any financial obligation, debt, claim or potential loss.

Taking the time to accurately fill in these forms will provide for you a full scope of your resources and the foundation from which you can determine the wisdom and affordability of future endeavors.

This PFS information should be updated each year. Keeping your personal financial statement up-to-date will help to accurately calculate your financial net worth. It will simplify the process of securing a loan or line of credit, should that need arise. It will provide a quick reference and index to identify assets and liabilities

The Personal Financial Statement form provided should meet the needs of most individuals. Utilize the back-up forms provided to record the details and specifics relating to your assets and liabilities. These forms will be helpful to you now and to everyone involved in your estate, after your death.

Forms 3 – 14

The first half of this chapter's assignment involves the following:

1. Creating a Personal Financial Statement (PFS) by utilizing either the form we provided or obtaining one from your bank, your accountant or on line.

2. Detail your assets and liabilities applying accurate appraisals and completing the forms provided.

3. Establish a system that reminds you to update this information annually.

4. Upon completion, place a copy of these forms in your Important Documents File. Establish a designated folder entitled Personal Financial Statement.

If you have any questions regarding how to fill out a personal financial statement you can go online and search "why fill out a personal financial statement" There are numerous sites offering instructions and answering specific questions.

What is our Current Budget?

I don't know about you, but personally I never really liked budgets. By nature budgets seem to be constraining. I built a career around sales. Sell enough and budgets don't matter. This works as long as times are good, sales are up and the team is winning. But what happens when sales slow down, the economy softens, the market turns, the product runs its course, numbers don't add up and time runs out? When budgets aren't established or adhered to, and expenses run greater than income, pressure mounts, changes are made, people lose jobs, businesses face closure and time becomes an adversary.

I recently asked a successful retailer in Colorado Springs to what he attributed the success of his company. His response wasn't what I expected: "I was taught that in good times you prepare for them to be bad, in bad times you prepare for them to be good."

My head visibly snapped back. Wait, say that again.

In good times you establish budgets, numbering things aright so that when bad times hit, you have the resources and time needed to make adjustments, sustain the storm and begin paving the way for good times. Wow! What an incredible approach and infrastructure! His grandfather taught him well. No matter what the current circumstances are, number your days aright and properly budget your resources.

One of the challenges of our time is very few neither people take the time nor exercise the discipline needed to establish a personal budget. Maybe that is because most budgets have the same success as diets. Both are commonly viewed as artificial constraints to be circumvented as the earliest opportunity. My accountant refers to budgeting as a project allocation of income and expenses. He tells me that clients seem to accept it better.

The "project allocation" or budgeting form that we have included in this chapter provides a tool to identify all the areas pulling from your finances. Our society, as a whole, is sadly lacking here and paying a huge price. The importance and the need in this area are exemplified by the numerous people who make and living and companies that exist to help people properly budget their finances.

What Do Casino Chips, Credit Cards and Paying Online Have in Common?

Using a credit card and paying online is a one-two punch that can be as dangerous as betting with chips in Vegas. The casinos figured it out. Playing with chips rather than real money numbs the effect of how much is being gambled. Swiping a card and authorizing direct withdrawals can have the same effect. It's quick, it's easy and you don't have to think about whether you have enough money in your wallet. It has been proven that paying with cash results in less spending. People who leave home without a credit card will spend 12% – 34% less monthly than they would if they were swiping plastic. It is not surprising that this generation is carrying more debt than any before it. The good news behind multiple credit cards and paying on line is you don't have to deal with the heaviness of budgeting…at least not initially. I am not opposed to credit cards or paying online. I use and do both. However, without discipline and without budgeting, they can be a negative force in piling up debt.

One of our employees shared with me that the first time she outlined her expenditures, she panicked and then quickly adopted a "budget-buy and save" philosophy. This caused her to look at all of her expenses carefully, deciding whether the purchase is a "need" or a "want." She set a budget in all areas of spending and included a plan for monthly savings.

The year our son got married, he and his wife Christy developed a spending diary. This took the form of an electronic spreadsheet. They entered everything they spent money on and exactly how much it cost. This is an eye-opening exercise. It is very easy to underestimate just how much money goes towards small things that aren't given much thought. A monthly spending diary will help you find out exactly where your money is going. After adjustments are considered, needed disciplines can be identified and then an accurate budget can be established. This is a fairly easy exercise that most people would greatly benefit from.

I learned in business school that proper budgeting involves an itemized summary of probable expenditures and probable income for a given period or project. It usually includes exact limits and specific plans for meeting expenses. Accountants would refer to this as "numbering things aright." My observation is that in business and personal affairs, exercising discipline in these areas helps lead to a heart of wisdom. Incorporating proper budgeting now will establish good habits and a template that will benefit your spouse and your family after you are gone.

Numbering our days aright has numerous tentacles and applications. Most involve budgeting both time and resources. The old adage comes to mind: failing to plan is planning to fail.

The Budget Barometer

Reviewing the categories of your expenditures provides a clear and unchallenged commentary on what things mean to you. Several years ago, a representative from a financial planning firm spoke at our CEO meeting. He stated that if anyone wanted help in discovering what was most important to them in life, all they had to do was give him their check book and credit card receipts. After reviewing the past year's expenditures he could tell anyone what their priorities were. We spend money and time in the direction of what matters most to us.

Re-Act vs. Pro-Act

All of us have had times when circumstances seemed to run us. If we stay in that mode too long we'll find that both time and resources have been squandered and wasted. Moses' prayer calls on God's help to pull him out of a reactive mode and into a pro-active mode. Begin with this prayer. Be still before God. Ask Him in desperation for a heart of wisdom. Ask Him for a fresh set of eyes as you review your current budget and re-establish one for the coming year. If you are married, involve your spouse. Discuss line items in detail. Pray together for wisdom and discipline.

Plan a budget that aligns with your needs, priorities, convictions and your hope. Then commit to employing the disciplines needed to apply your decisions.

Current Budget Worksheet
Form 15

The final step in this chapter involves planning your current estimated budget. For greatest effectiveness, actual expenditures should be reviewed monthly and this form then updated twice a year, with proper time set aside to review actual expenditures vs. budget. As mentioned earlier, if you aren't currently working with a budget, the numbers associated with some of the line items will surprise you. Take the time needed. Establish historical accuracy. You will then be properly prepared to make adjustments and establish a workable budget. Review this every six months. Adjust as needed.

As part of your over-all strategic planning, Chapter 4 will address your *estimated future budget* involving Social Security benefits, company retirement benefits and income, impact upon a loss of a spouse and insurance benefits.

For now, stay focused on what is current. Work to establish a realistic budget.

Personal Financial Statement
(Update annually)

FORM 3

Updated: _____

ASSETS (PRESENT MARKET VALUE)	
Cash on hand:	
Checking account:	
Savings / money market:	
Stocks / bonds / mutual funds:	
Cash value of life insurance:	
Coins:	
Collectibles and Memorabilia:	
Real Estate (Home):	
Other real estate:	
Loans / Notes receivable:	
Business valuation:	
Automobiles / other vehicles:	
Furniture:	
Jewelry:	
Other personal property:	
IRA / 401k:	
Pension / retirement plan:	
Other assets:	
Other assets:	
Other assets:	
TOTAL	$

LIABILITIES (CURRENT AMOUNT OWED)	
Home mortgage:	
Automobile loans:	
Credit card debt:	
Other real estate mortgages:	
Personal debts to relatives / friends:	
Bank loans:	
Business loans:	
Educational loans:	
Medical:	
Other past due bills:	
Life insurance loans:	
Other debts and loans:	
Other debts and loans:	
Other debts and loans:	
TOTAL LIAB	$
NET (total assets less to	$

(41)

Real Estate

FORM 4

Updated: _____

Location of Property:	
Deed in Name(s) of:	
Purchase Price:	
Purchase Date:	
Location of Deed:	
Assessed Value:	Land:　　　　　　　Building: Total:
Other Taxes / Assessments Due:	Payee: Amount:　　　　　　Date Payable:
Mortgage Holder:	
Mortgage Satisfaction location: *(if fully paid)*	
Lease/Rental agreement location: *(if rental property)*	
Terms of lease/rental agreement:	

Location of Property:	
Deed in Name(s) of:	
Purchase Price:	
Purchase Date:	
Location of Deed:	
Assessed Value:	Land:　　　　　　　Building: Total:
Other Taxes / Assessments Due:	Payee: Amount:　　　　　　Date Payable:
Mortgage Holder:	
Mortgage Satisfaction location: *(if fully paid)*	
Lease/Rental agreement location: *(if rental property)*	
Terms of lease/rental agreement:	

Automobiles and Other Vehicles

(Place a copy of each vehicle's title and registration form in this workbook)

FORM 5

Updated: _____

Description of Vehicle:	Make:	Model:
	Body Type/Color:	
Purchasing Information:	Date:	Cost:
Registered Owner:		
Owner's Address:		
License Plate:	Number:	State:
Vehicle Identification #:		
First Lien Holder:		
Second Lien Holder:		
Vehicle Title Located:		

Description of Vehicle:	Make:	Model:
	Body Type/Color:	
Purchasing Information:	Date:	Cost:
Registered Owner:		
Owner's Address:		
License Plate:	Number:	State:
Vehicle Identification #:		
First Lien Holder:		
Second Lien Holder:		
Vehicle Title Located:		

Description of Vehicle:	Make:	Model:
	Body Type/Color:	
Purchasing Information:	Date:	Cost:
Registered Owner:		
Owner's Address:		
License Plate:	Number:	State:
Vehicle Identification #:		
First Lien Holder:		
Second Lien Holder:		
Vehicle Title Located:		

Valuable Personal Property

(Please ask your insurance agent to determine if these items are properly covered in your household or other insurance policies and if the coverage reflects current values. Attach photocopies of any appraisals.)

FORM 6

Updated: _____

DESCRIPTIONS AND ESTIMATED VALUES OF SOME OF OUR MOST VALUABLE PROPERTY

Description of Property: _____
Estimated Value: $ _____ Date Valued: _____ Appraised: ○Y ○N

Description of Property: _____
Estimated Value: $ _____ Date Valued: _____ Appraised: ○Y ○N

Description of Property: _____
Estimated Value: $ _____ Date Valued: _____ Appraised: ○Y ○N

Description of Property: _____
Estimated Value: $ _____ Date Valued: _____ Appraised: ○Y ○N

Description of Property: _____
Estimated Value: $ _____ Date Valued: _____ Appraised: ○Y ○N

Description of Property: _____
Estimated Value: $ _____ Date Valued: _____ Appraised: ○Y ○N

Description of Property: _____
Estimated Value: $ _____ Date Valued: _____ Appraised: ○Y ○N

Description of Property: _____
Estimated Value: $ _____ Date Valued: _____ Appraised: ○Y ○N

Description of Property: _____
Estimated Value: $ _____ Date Valued: _____ Appraised: ○Y ○N

Description of Property: _____
Estimated Value: $ _____ Date Valued: _____ Appraised: ○Y ○N

Description of Property: _____
Estimated Value: $ _____ Date Valued: _____ Appraised: ○Y ○N

Description of Property: _____
Estimated Value: $ _____ Date Valued: _____ Appraised: ○Y ○N

Description of Property: _____
Estimated Value: $ _____ Date Valued: _____ Appraised: ○Y ○N

Stocks Held
(Note: Most stocks are held in brokerage accounts and do not need to be listed separately)

FORM 7

Updated: _____

BROKERAGE INFORMATION	
Brokerage Firm:	
Account Number:	
Contact Person:	
Address:	
Phone:	
E-mail Address:	
Approximate Value:	

Additional stocks not held at brokerage firm

Stock Description:			
Number of Shares:		Dividend Information:	
Date Acquired:		Purchase Price:	
Where Held:		Other Information:	

Stock Description:			
Number of Shares:		Dividend Information:	
Date Acquired:		Purchase Price:	
Where Held:		Other Information:	

Stock Description:			
Number of Shares:		Dividend Information:	
Date Acquired:		Purchase Price:	
Where Held:		Other Information:	

Stock Description:			
Number of Shares:		Dividend Information:	
Date Acquired:		Purchase Price:	
Where Held:		Other Information:	

Stock Description:			
Number of Shares:		Dividend Information:	
Date Acquired:		Purchase Price:	
Where Held:		Other Information:	

Bonds Held

FORM 8

Updated: _____

Bond Description:	
Face Amount:	Yield:	Maturity Date:
Date Acquired:	Purchase Price:
Where Held:	Other Information:

Bond Description:	
Face Amount:	Yield:	Maturity Date:
Date Acquired:	Purchase Price:
Where Held:	Other Information:

Bond Description:	
Face Amount:	Yield:	Maturity Date:
Date Acquired:	Purchase Price:
Where Held:	Other Information:

Bond Description:	
Face Amount:	Yield:	Maturity Date:
Date Acquired:	Purchase Price:
Where Held:	Other Information:

Bond Description:	
Face Amount:	Yield:	Maturity Date:
Date Acquired:	Purchase Price:
Where Held:	Other Information:

Bond Description:	
Face Amount:	Yield:	Maturity Date:
Date Acquired:	Purchase Price:
Where Held:	Other Information:

Bond Description:	
Face Amount:	Yield:	Maturity Date:
Date Acquired:	Purchase Price:
Where Held:	Other Information:

Other Investments

FORM 9

Updated: _____

Name / Description:	
(If applicable) Contact:	Phone:
Contact Address:	
Date Acquired:	Purchase Price:

Name / Description:	
(If applicable) Contact:	Phone:
Contact Address:	
Date Acquired:	Purchase Price:

Name / Description:	
(If applicable) Contact:	Phone:
Contact Address:	
Date Acquired:	Purchase Price:

Name / Description:	
(If applicable) Contact:	Phone:
Contact Address:	
Date Acquired:	Purchase Price:

Name / Description:	
(If applicable) Contact:	Phone:
Contact Address:	
Date Acquired:	Purchase Price:

Name / Description:	
(If applicable) Contact:	Phone:
Contact Address:	
Date Acquired:	Purchase Price:

Name / Description:	
(If applicable) Contact:	Phone:
Contact Address:	
Date Acquired:	Purchase Price:

Receivables

FORM 10

Updated: _____

Debtor's Name:	Phone:
Address:	Loan Amt:
Terms of Payment:	
Add'l Terms/Info:	

Debtor's Name:	Phone:
Address:	Loan Amt:
Terms of Payment:	
Add'l Terms/Info:	

Debtor's Name:	Phone:
Address:	Loan Amt:
Terms of Payment:	
Add'l Terms/Info:	

Debtor's Name:	Phone:
Address:	Loan Amt:
Terms of Payment:	
Add'l Terms/Info:	

Debtor's Name:	Phone:
Address:	Loan Amt:
Terms of Payment:	
Add'l Terms/Info:	

Debtor's Name:	Phone:
Address:	Loan Amt:
Terms of Payment:	
Add'l Terms/Info:	

Debtor's Name:	Phone:
Address:	Loan Amt:
Terms of Payment:	
Add'l Terms/Info:	

Additional Key Assets

FORM 11

Updated: _____

Item / Description:	
Date Purchased:	Value:

Item / Description:	
Date Purchased:	Value:

Item / Description:	
Date Purchased:	Value:

Item / Description:	
Date Purchased:	Value:

Item / Description:	
Date Purchased:	Value:

Item / Description:	
Date Purchased:	Value:

Item / Description:	
Date Purchased:	Value:

Item / Description:	
Date Purchased:	Value:

Item / Description:	
Date Purchased:	Value:

Item / Description:	
Date Purchased:	Value:

Item / Description:	
Date Purchased:	Value:

Item / Description:	
Date Purchased:	Value:

Item / Description:	
Date Purchased:	Value:

Debt Details

FORM 12

Updated: _____

CREDITOR	PURCHASE	MONTHLY PAYMENT	BALANCE DUE	PAY-OFF DATE	INTEREST RATE	PAYMENTS PAST DUE
		Total: $	$			

AUTOMOBILE LOANS

		Total Automobile Loans: $	$			

HOME MORTGAGES

		Total Home Mortgages: $	$			

PERSONAL AND BUSINESS INVESTMENTS / DEBT

		Total Investments/Debt: $	$			
		TOTAL DEBT: $	$			

Credit Cards

FORM 13

Updated: _____

Card Issuer:		APR:	
Account Number:		Balance:	
Authorized Signer(s):			
Call if Lost/Stolen:		Password:	

Card Issuer:		APR:	
Account Number:		Balance:	
Authorized Signer(s):			
Call if Lost/Stolen:		Password:	

Card Issuer:		APR:	
Account Number:		Balance:	
Authorized Signer(s):			
Call if Lost/Stolen:		Password:	

Card Issuer:		APR:	
Account Number:		Balance:	
Authorized Signer(s):			
Call if Lost/Stolen:		Password:	

Card Issuer:		APR:	
Account Number:		Balance:	
Authorized Signer(s):			
Call if Lost/Stolen:		Password:	

Card Issuer:		APR:	
Account Number:		Balance:	
Authorized Signer(s):			
Call if Lost/Stolen:		Password:	

Card Issuer:		APR:	
Account Number:		Balance:	
Authorized Signer(s):			
Call if Lost/Stolen:		Password:	

Bank Accounts

FORM 14

Updated: _____

Account Name:	Account #:
Financial Institution:	
Account Type:	○ *Checking* ○ *Savings* ○ *Business* ○ *Interest-bearing* ○ *Other:*
Joint Account:	○ *Y* ○ *N* Co-holder:
Checkbook Located:	
PIN #:	Password:

Account Name:	Account #:
Financial Institution:	
Account Type:	○ *Checking* ○ *Savings* ○ *Business* ○ *Interest-bearing* ○ *Other:*
Joint Account:	○ *Y* ○ *N* Co-holder:
Checkbook Located:	
PIN #:	Password:

Account Name:	Account #:
Financial Institution:	
Account Type:	○ *Checking* ○ *Savings* ○ *Business* ○ *Interest-bearing* ○ *Other:*
Joint Account:	○ *Y* ○ *N* Co-holder:
Checkbook Located:	
PIN #:	Password:

Account Name:	Account #:
Financial Institution:	
Account Type:	○ *Checking* ○ *Savings* ○ *Business* ○ *Interest-bearing* ○ *Other:*
Joint Account:	○ *Y* ○ *N* Co-holder:
Checkbook Located:	
PIN #:	Password:

Account Name:	Account #:
Financial Institution:	
Account Type:	○ *Checking* ○ *Savings* ○ *Business* ○ *Interest-bearing* ○ *Other:*
Joint Account:	○ *Y* ○ *N* Co-holder:
Checkbook Located:	
PIN #:	Password:

Current Estimated Budget

(Update semi-annually)

FORM 15

Updated: _____

	GROSS MONTHLY INCOME:	$	8	**RECREATION:**	$
	Salary:			Eating Out:	
	Interest:			Memberships:	
	Dividends:			Activities:	
	Other:			Vacation:	
	Other:			Hobbies:	
Less				Other:	
1	Charitable Giving:		9	**CLOTHING:**	$
2	Federal Tax:		10	**SAVINGS:**	$
	State Tax:			Personal:	
	FICA:			Educational:	
	NET SPENDABLE INCOME:	$		Retirement:	
			11	**MEDICAL:**	$
3	**HOUSING:**	$		Doctor(s):	
	Mortgage (or rent):			Dentist:	
	Insurance:			Rx Drugs:	
	Taxes:			Other:	
	Electricity:		12	**MISCELLANEOUS:**	$
	Gas:			Cable / Internet:	
	Water:			Toiletries, Cosmetics	
	Sanitation:			Beauty Shop / Barber:	
	Telephone:			Laundry / Dry-cleaning:	
	Maintenance:			Allowances, Lunches:	
	Other:			Subscriptions:	
	Other:			Gifts (inc. Christmas):	
4	**FOOD / GROCERIES:**	$		Decorating:	
5	**AUTOMOBILE:**	$		Other:	
	Payments:			Other:	
	Gas / Oil:		13	**INVESTMENTS:**	$
	Insurance:		14	**SCHOOL / CHILD CARE:**	$
	License / Taxes:			Tuition:	
	Maintenance / Repair:			Supplies:	
6	**INSURANCE:**	$		Clothing:	
	Life:			Transportation:	
	Medical:			Day Care:	
	Other:			Other:	
7	**DEBTS:**	$		**TOTAL EXPENSES:**	$
	Credit Card:				
	Loans / Notes:			**INCOME VERSUS EXPENSES**	
	Other:			Net Spendable Income:	
	Other:			Less Expenses:	
				UNALLOCATED SURPLUS:	$

(65)

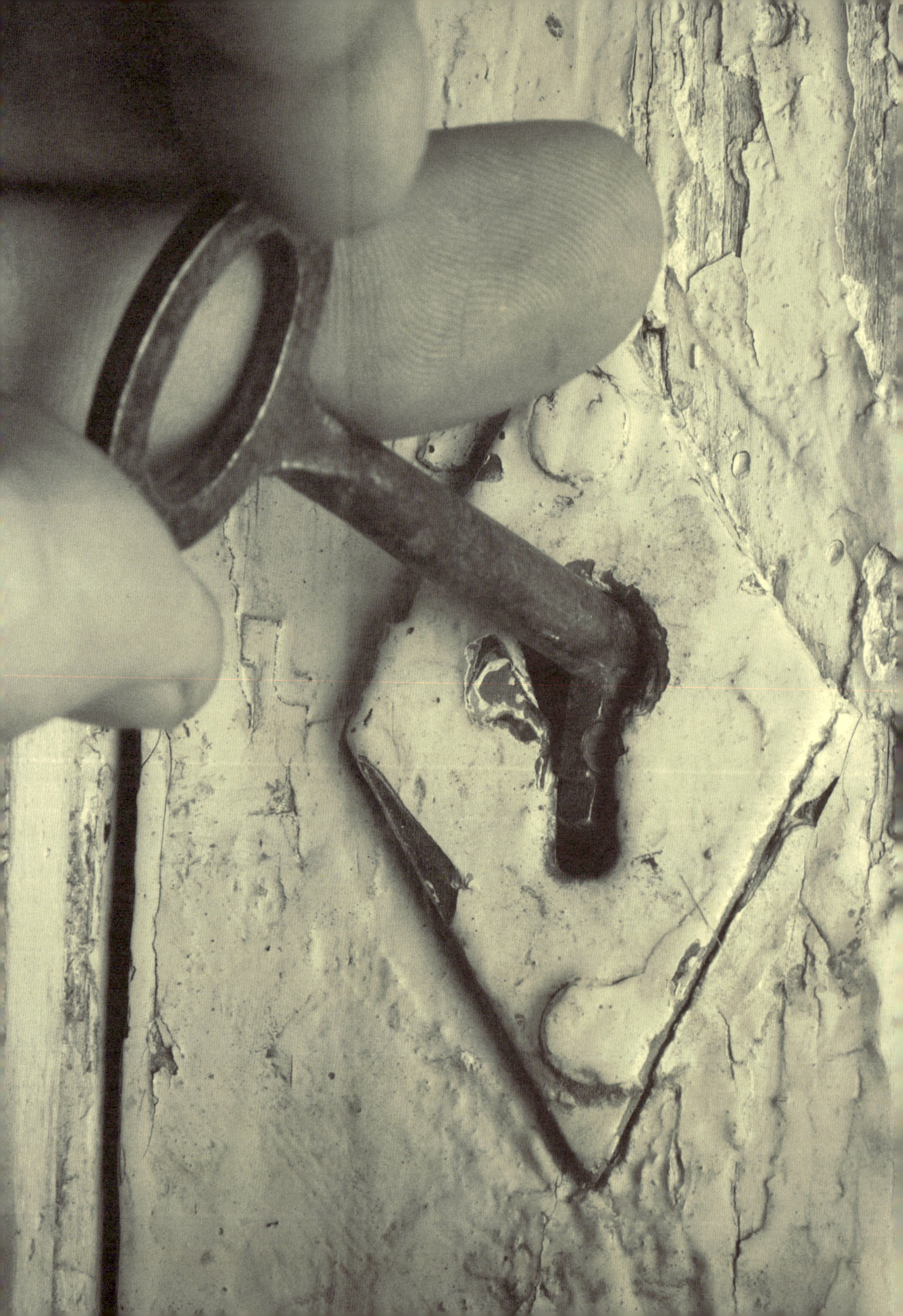

CHAPTER 4

From *Meaning* to *Knowledge*

What Do Others Need to Know?

My brother-in-law Frank recently told me a story about an incredible water heater, the type that anyone would appreciate as an inclusion with a new home purchase. He explained that his aunt had recently died and while he was cleaning out the house in preparation for putting it up for sale, he and his family kept finding hidden wads of money. The water heater, it turned out, provided more than just hot baths. It was also the hiding place for eight hundred dollars of cold, hard cash strapped to the back side. That wasn't all: a shoe box in the closet coughed up three hundred more. Five hundred dollars were hidden in the basement rafters. Ten twenties were nesting in the flower jar.

Frank and his family spent hours exploring every possible hiding place they could think of. As he told the story, my mind began to think of the pleasant surprises that will await the next owner should they discover any additional hiding places. There is no telling what might be buried in the garden.

The Hiding Place

We all seem to have them. Special hiding places. An outside key hidden in a planter or placed on top of the porch pillar. Letters and money under the mattress. Jewelry tucked away in the underwear drawer. Police will tell you professional thieves know that most people put their valuables in the top or bottom drawer of their dresser. It is common for those two drawers only to be pulled out and turned over as burglars move quickly to get in and out of a house.

(67)

The hiding places for cash and valuables in many homes have become more sophisticated. Books with cut out sections of pages provide a hollow hiding place. Cans that look like they would contain tennis balls or pet food. Insulation in the attic can provide a safe place and for the mechanically minded, removing light switch plates provides an undetected cavity. A favorite for centuries involves hollowing out a place within a piece of wooden furniture.

I read an article a while back that highlighted the top five ways to create a secure hiding place in your home:

- Inside the walls, particularly behind hanging clothes
- Add ceiling or wall beams as an architectural feature and make one false with a hidden compartment
- Create a hollowed storage area behind a baseboard
- Behind a full length mirror on a door or on a wall
- Under the bottom shelf of a bookcase.

All of these are great ideas. The question, regardless of where we put our things, is who do we tell? When do we tell them? How do we best reveal our hiding places? What happens if this knowledge goes undetected?

These questions pertain to the stuff we hide. But we must also apply these questions to the information we hide. In today's world, everyone seems to have Personal Identification Numbers on multiple accounts. In addition there are passwords to information on computers, access codes and pin numbers that need to be recorded.

My wife flew to Wisconsin this past summer to attend her uncle's funeral. He died very unexpectedly. As Sandy, her mother and sister maneuvered through his estate, they bumped against numerous obstacles. Seemingly simple things like canceling Direct TV could not be accomplished without a pin number. It remained active until they could fax a copy of his death certificate.

People Don't Know What they Don't Know

ABC News ran a story disclosing that 50 states are holding more than $32 billion worth of unclaimed property including jewelry, cash and un-cashed checks seized from safety deposit boxes. The state of Illinois holds a "Silver and Gold" sale each year during the weeks leading into Christmas. This year, over $125,000 worth of various items like diamonds, pearl necklaces, wedding rings, earrings, watches and even four Mickey Mantle baseball cards are listed on eBay. All of these items were seized from bank deposit boxes not visited for 10 years.

The bottom line is: People don't know what they don't know because it remains outside their line of view. Consequently, tremendous value from countless estates goes unclaimed, and up for auction or remains unfound and wasted.

Documentation

The forms you completed in the previous chapter provided a snapshot of your current financial picture through two different lenses. In the current budget, you captured your earnings, obligations and cash flow. In other words, you looked at your finances inside a 30-day window. Secondly, you took inventory of your assets and liabilities. Assets and liabilities are more permanent fixtures to your portfolio.

On the surface this would appear to be a complete rendering of your over-all current financial status. But for many, there are still some things hidden from view.

Some things we hide from view intentionally. The reason we do this is to restrict access. When we consider something valuable, we naturally want to protect it. What better way to protect something than to move it outside of others' line of view. Generally speaking, there are two things we hide: information and stuff. When objects and information sit outside the scope of our perspective, they can get lost. Family doesn't know these things exist, so they won't even know to look for them.

Forms 16 – 22

The first grouping of forms in this chapter will assist you in documenting information relating to home safes, safety deposit boxes at your bank, hidden items of value, things loaned to others and electronic pass codes and pin numbers. Fill these out first and then we will move forward with the communication of practical information surrounding your affairs. As with all sections, take time to expand and customize the list we provide until it is complete.

How To Keep Things Going...

I am often amazed by the various topics that are researched. I read recently of a study that was done examining how couples begin to look more and more alike, the longer they are together. Researchers handed out separate pictures of men and women and asked a panel to match the couples. The panel, comprised of 10 men and 10 women, correctly matched over 80% of the 160 marriages. It was surmised that the longer a couple is together, the more they begin to look alike. It was further concluded that common activities, surroundings and emotional experiences all play into this.

Apparently, given enough time, couples start looking somewhat the same. It is also true that as time goes on marriage partners take on specific roles. Each marriage is different, but whatever role each partner assumes, they generally keep it throughout the marriage. Quickly survey in your mind the number of functions you fill in your home that no one else in your family would have the first clue how to perform. Jot a few of these down and then reverse it. How many functions does your spouse fulfill that you would be lost in performing until someone educated you on how to do it?

If I was no longer here, what do you wish I would have told you about or taken the time to explain?

When your spouse dies, your whole world changes. There is a time of emotional adjustment that is very difficult to get through. One of the objectives for Unfinished Business is to try and help eliminate as many of the small aggravations as possible. Specifically, the aggravations connected with not knowing how to do certain things or who to contact when there is a problem or where something as simple as the water shut off valve is located.

As I pointed out earlier, each of the men in our IRON group asked our wife: "If I was no longer here, what do you wish I would have told you about or taken the time to explain?

The remaining forms in this section were developed as a result of the responses we received from our wives. They cover numerous household things as well as guidelines on whom to talk with when your spouse or family are facing certain decisions..

Forms 23 – 28

These forms are not comprehensive. Each marriage is different. Refer back to the answers you received from your spouse to the questions in Chapter 1. Add personalized pages of your own to a file entitled "How To Keep Things Going." Set out to complete information that fits your particular roles and circumstances. It will take a little bit of your time to put this together, but someday it will help make things a whole lot easier for those that you love.

Practical Advisors
Forms 29 – 31

The final grouping of forms in this chapter relates to practical advisors. Good advice is even harder to find than money strapped to a water heater or a diamond ring sitting behind the light switch plate.

Stranger in a Strange Land

Think of the last time you were a stranger in a strange land. Earlier this year I was asked to attend a strategy meeting to help provide counsel to a friend who was considering selling his business. I was the "new guy" in the room and didn't know anyone except the owner of the business who had invited me. Before things got started, I worked my way around the conference table and during the few moments of introductions I was recognized as Rachel's father and Tim's father-in-law. Two of the men in the room were on the board where Tim and Rachel work. Wham! Just like that, the dynamic changed. I went from being an outsider to having instant connection. This is an example of transferred relationship.

A few months ago, I was in the market for new tires. Talk about a stranger in a strange land. I stopped in a tire shop on the way home from the office and left double checking the landscape to make sure I hadn't stepped back in time or into a 1920's gangster flick. The next day, I shared the experience with my son, Ryan, who enjoys customizing cars and has been involved in several auto shows. He called the owner of a tire and rim shop across town. Immediately I was given VIP service and treated like family. Once again, a transferred relationship changed an uncomfortable scenario into an enjoyable purchase.

The question here is: what relationships do you have that your family can benefit from? How can you transfer your relationships to help your family both now and when you are gone?

As we go through life, we form certain relationships that add value, provide meaning and make life easier. We learn by experience who is reliable, who has certain areas of expertise and who we can trust for good, solid, practical advice. We form relationship with people who are competent in their field. They know things we don't know and see things we don't see. We need them in our life and appreciate them every time they apply their expertise to our situation.

Don't hide these relationships. Take time to list everyone who comes to mind. Focus on those with practical applications. In the next chapter we will be making a similar list of those who can speak wise counsel into life's various challenges.

Chances are, most of the areas of your practical responsibilities at home are intimidating to your spouse. If they are not intimidating they certainly present challenges. You have already worked your way through most of the challenges and issues. You have relationships in the areas of automobiles, tires, home maintenance and finance that will be extremely beneficial to your family.

From your perspective many of these things are easy, but from the perspective of your mate; they may have no standard or base line from which to gauge what is fair and what is right. I explained the concept of *Unfinished Business* to a widow who works in the administrative offices at a condo on Sanibel Island where Sandy and I have vacationed the past several years. She explained that she suddenly lost her husband two years ago and went on to say, "You have no idea how much something like this would have helped me. I relied on him for just about everything and have had to learn and teach myself every aspect of day-to-day life. It has been very difficult."

One of the best things you can do for your spouse and for your family is share contacts and information. Over the years, we establish some very meaningful and trustworthy relationships. Begin by documenting the names of the people you have relied on and found to be honest and accurate. Utilize the forms provided as a guideline and file this information in your Important Documents filing system. Continue this process by taking time to introduce these individuals to your family, both on paper, and as much as possible, in person.

Ask yourself this: what would it look like to host a backyard cook-out that included your family as well as the families of everyone you rely on for practical help? Your neighbors and friends might buy a ticket to a networking dinner like that!

Much of the information that you document in this chapter may seem mundane to you, but it will be extremely valuable to those left behind. Keep them clearly in mind as you share your knowledge, and work your way through forms 16 – 31. The information and knowledge you leave will be priceless.

General Information

FORM 16

Updated: _____

I [○ DO] [○ DO NOT] have a safe deposit box.

It can be found at: _____

The key can be found at: _____

The following people have signature authority on the box:

_____

_____

_____

_____

I [○ DO] [○ DO NOT] have a safe.

The combination is: _____

The safe can be found: _____

The password to my computer is: _____

My email address is: _____

My internet account is with: _____

Other important passwords and PIN numbers include:

ITEM, PROGRAM, SERVICE COMPANY OR BANK	ACCESS	PASSWORD / PIN #

(73)

Safe-Deposit Box 1 – Inventory

FORM 17

Updated: _____

Location:	
Key Location:	Box #:
Financial Institution:	
City, State, Zip:	
Phone:	Fax:
Authorized Signers:	

Description of Inventory

Birth Certificates:	
Marriage Certificates:	
Social Security Cards:	
Military Discharges:	
Wills:	
Trusts:	
Deeds:	
Mortgages:	
Leases:	
Business Agreements:	
Investment Documents:	
Automobile Titles:	
Power of Attorney:	
Insurance Policies:	

(75)

Safe-Deposit Box 2 – Inventory

FORM 18

Updated: _____

Location:	
Key Location:	Box #:
Financial Institution:	
City, State, Zip:	
Phone:	Fax:
Authorized Signers:	

Description of Inventory

Birth Certificates:	
Marriage Certificates:	
Social Security Cards:	
Military Discharges:	
Wills:	
Trusts:	
Deeds:	
Mortgages:	
Leases:	
Business Agreements:	
Investment Documents:	
Automobile Titles:	
Power of Attorney:	
Insurance Policies:	

(77)

Home Safe / File Cabinet – Inventory

FORM 19

Updated: _____

Location:	
Key Location:	
Combination:	
DESCRIPTION OF INVENTORY	
Birth Certificates:	
Marriage Certificates:	
Social Security Cards:	
Military Discharges:	
Wills:	
Trusts:	
Deeds:	
Mortgages:	
Leases:	
Business Agreements:	
Investment Documents:	
Automobile Titles:	
Power of Attorney:	
Insurance Policies:	

(79)

Items Loaned to Others

Updated: _____

We have loaned the following items to others:

Item:	Loan Date:	Return Date:
Loaned to:		Phone:

Item:	Loan Date:	Return Date:
Loaned to:		Phone:

Item:	Loan Date:	Return Date:
Loaned to:		Phone:

Item:	Loan Date:	Return Date:
Loaned to:		Phone:

Item:	Loan Date:	Return Date:
Loaned to:		Phone:

Item:	Loan Date:	Return Date:
Loaned to:		Phone:

Item:	Loan Date:	Return Date:
Loaned to:		Phone:

Item:	Loan Date:	Return Date:
Loaned to:		Phone:

Item:	Loan Date:	Return Date:
Loaned to:		Phone:

Item:	Loan Date:	Return Date:
Loaned to:		Phone:

Item:	Loan Date:	Return Date:
Loaned to:		Phone:

Item:	Loan Date:	Return Date:
Loaned to:		Phone:

Item:	Loan Date:	Return Date:
Loaned to:		Phone:

Computer Instructions

FORM 21

Updated: _____

Location(s) of Computer(s): _____

Password(s): _____

Name(s) of programs containing IMPORTANT INFORMATION	Name(s) of programs containing OTHER INFORMATION

Person(s) familiar with our computer and programs who can retrieve what is needed

Name: _____
Company Name: _____
Address: _____
Phone: _____

Name: _____
Company Name: _____
Address: _____
Phone: _____

(83)

Hidden Items of Value

(List valuable items that you have stored or hidden in places other than your home safe or a safe deposit box.)   Updated:

Item	Location

Helpful Household Answers

FORM 23

Updated: _____

Home Address:		Phone:	
Neighbor's Name:		Home Phone:	
Address:		Work Phone:	
		Cell Phone:	
Relative's Name:		Home Phone:	
Address:		Work Phone:	
		Cell Phone:	

LOCATION OF

Alarm System Box:		Thermostat(s):	
Circuit Breaker Box:		Air Filter(s):	
Extra House Key(s):		Water Cut-off:	
Fire Extinguisher(s):		Other:	
Paint Cans Exterior:		Other:	
Paint Cans Interior:		Other:	
Screens for Doors:		Other:	
Window Screens:		Other:	

HELPFUL NAMES AND NUMBERS

Air/Heating:		Phone:	
Alarm Company:		Phone:	
Appliance Repair:		Phone:	
Clergy:		Phone:	
Dentist:		Phone:	
Doctor(s):		Phone:	
Drug Store:		Phone:	
Electrician:		Phone:	
Fire Department:		Phone:	
Hospital:		Phone:	
Plumber:		Phone:	
Police Department:		Phone:	
Veterinarian:		Phone:	
Other:		Phone:	
Other:		Phone:	
Other:		Phone:	

Household Mechanics Overview
(Include helpful notes regarding operation and maintenance)

FORM 24

Updated: _____

ITEMS
Furnace:
Air Conditioning:
Water Heaters:
Electronics/Audio-Visual Systems:
Fireplace:
Grill:
Water Purifier:
Garbage Disposal:
Air Humidifier:
Clean Air System:
Outdoor Lighting:
Yard Irrigation:
Electronic Fence (for dog(s), if applicable):
Other:

Note: For a complete listing of Spring and full home maintenance Google "Household Maintenance Checklist."

(89)

Household Appliances
(Include operating and maintenance instructions)

FORM 25

Updated: _____

ITEMS

Washer:

Dryer:

Oven:

Stove Top:

Refrigerator:

Microwave:

Dishwasher:

Other Appliances:

Neighborhood Directory

(Attach a copy of your neighborhood directory; highlight neighbors with whom you have a close relationship)   Updated: _____

Neighbor List

Automotive Strategy

FORM 27

Updated: _____

Automobiles represent one of the largest on-going expenditures in household budgeting. Following is my recommendation on when and how to approach the decision involving leasing or buying, new or used, what kind, how much, when and who to take advice from.

RECOMMENDATION

MAINTENANCE GUIDELINES

Purchasing Decisions

FORM 28

Updated: _____

Whether the budget is very tight and there doesn't seem to be enough funds to go around or the savings account is large, eliminating financial pressures, proper decision-making processes should be followed in order to be good stewards of our resources. Following is my recommendation or template to follow when making small and large purchasing decisions.

RECOMMENDATION

Small items, those defined as $_____ and below:

_____
_____
_____
_____
_____
_____
_____
_____
_____
_____

Large items, those defined as $_____ and above:

_____
_____
_____
_____
_____
_____
_____
_____
_____
_____

Key Practical Advisors

FORM 29

Updated: _____

ATTORNEY	
Name:	
Name of Firm:	
Street Address:	
City, State, Zip:	
Phone:	
Cell:	
Fax:	
Email Address:	
Area of Strength:	

ACCOUNTANT	
Name:	
Name of Firm:	
Street Address:	
City, State, Zip:	
Phone:	
Cell:	
Fax:	
Email Address:	

FINANCIAL ADVISOR	
Name:	
Name of Company:	
Street Address:	
City, State, Zip:	
Phone:	
Cell:	
Fax:	
Email Address:	

Key Practical Advisors

FORM 30

Updated: ....

INSURANCE AGENT

Name:	
Name of Agency:	
Street Address:	
City, State, Zip:	
Phone:	
Cell:	
Fax:	
Email Address:	

REAL ESTATE ADVISOR

Name:	
Name of Brokerage:	
Street Address:	
City, State, Zip:	
Phone:	
Cell:	
Fax:	
Email Address:	

BANKER

Name:	
Name of Bank:	
Street Address:	
City, State, Zip:	
Phone:	
Cell:	
Fax:	
Email Address:	

Key Practical Advisors

FORM 31

Updated: _____

OTHER
Name:
Relationship/Organization:
Street Address:
City, State, Zip:
Phone:
Cell:
Fax:
Email Address:

OTHER
Name:
Relationship/Organization:
Street Address:
City, State, Zip:
Phone:
Cell:
Fax:
Email Address:

OTHER
Name:
Relationship/Organization:
Street Address:
City, State, Zip:
Phone:
Cell:
Fax:
Email Address:

(103)

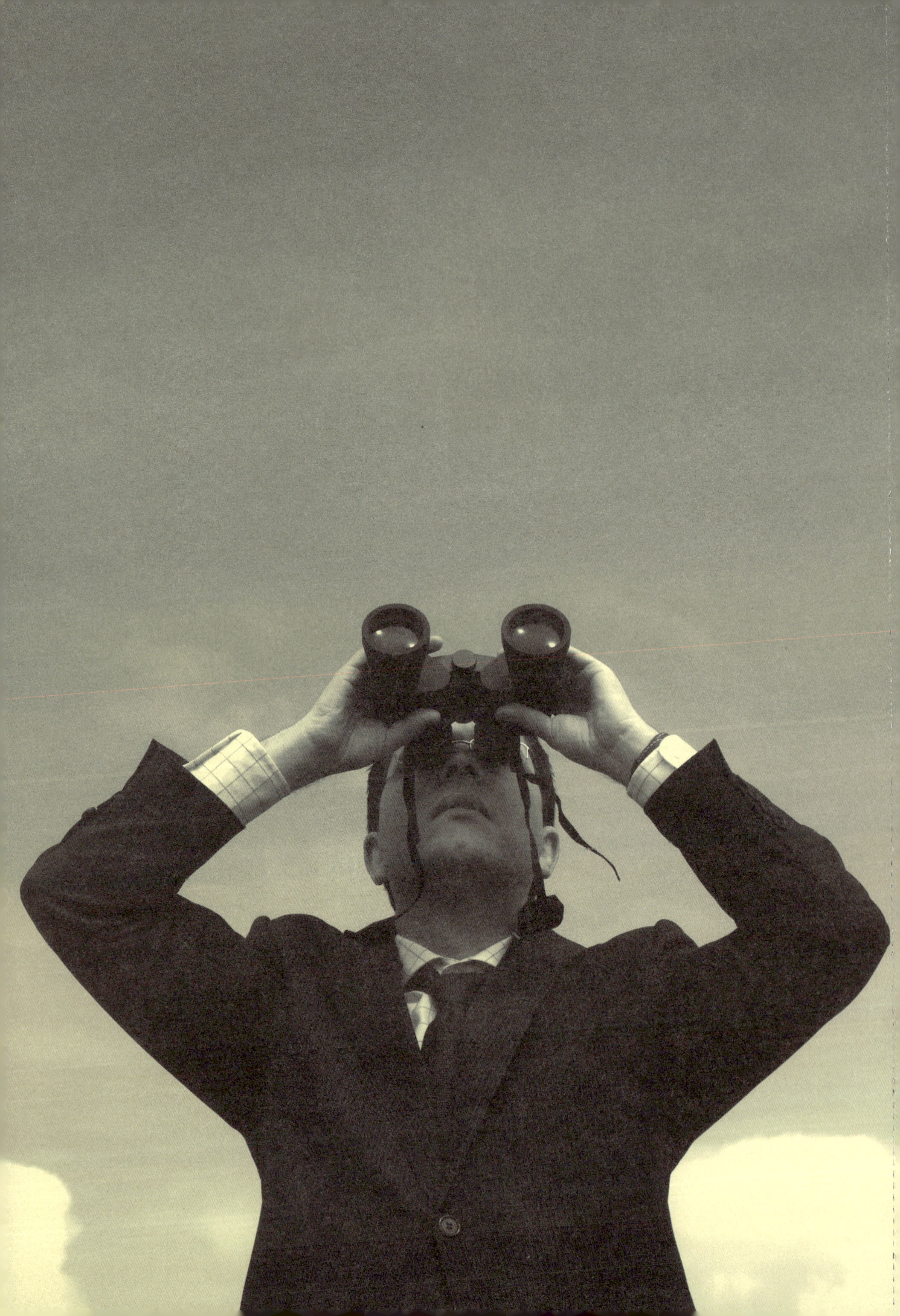

CHAPTER 5

From *Knowledge* to *Wisdom*

CONNECTING THE SHIFTING DOTS

*"Blessed is the man who finds wisdom,
and the man who gains understanding,
for its profit is greater than that of silver
and its gain than fine gold.
She is more precious than jewels,
and nothing I desire can compare with her.
Long life is in her right hand;
in her left hand are riches and honor.
Her ways are pleasant ways,
and all her paths are peace.
She is a tree of life to those who embrace her,
and happy are those who hold her fast.".*

KING SOLOMON
PROVERBS 3:13-18

Do you know what the best bargain in the marketplace is? Many great business leaders would say that it is wise input and advice. Companies and individuals often get themselves in trouble and set themselves up for failure or to be taken advantage of if they make decisions and move forward in unfamiliar areas without first getting input and wise counsel.

Long ago, Solomon wrote, "Where there is no counsel, the people fall; but in the multitude of counselors there is safety." Proverbs 11:14

This past week, I met with a friend who opened his own business five years ago. Every indication is that he will be forced to close and he will likely file bankruptcy. What happened? He is a very bright guy with two decades of experience in his industry. He knew a lot about some of the pieces necessary to succeed, but he wasn't experienced in others and didn't slow down or seek counsel in his areas of weakness. He told me that if he could do it all over again he would establish his own advisory board, be much more open regarding his areas of deficiency and never stop learning.

Six years ago, I was introduced to Gayle Jackson. In reality it was more of an interview than an introduction. I wasn't the one asking the questions. Gayle had a long and successful career as an IBM executive. As his career with them was winding down, he left and started his own technology business. He is street smart, savvy and gritty and has experienced things that still lay ahead of me. Today, he is my mentor. Four decades earlier, he met Walt Henrichsen. Walt is his mentor. Together, they have explored the truths, mysteries and applications of God's Word. They have studied together, written books, held conferences, spoken at retreats and invested in the lives of thousands of men, exhorting toward a closer walk with God. That is a big part of what they do. Invest in men. They provide wisdom, give counsel and they share relationships.

I remember leaving that first meeting at IHOP knowing that what just happened in that booth was the first step in a journey that would impact my life. Two weeks later I attended my first R12:2 CEO meeting. Gayle leads this group. He introduced the guest speaker and explained that one of the best things he will do for us is share his relationships. This is a network of guys with tremendous substance and various areas of expertise. They have been part of his life. As we have met through the years at our R:12:2 meeting, he has brought them in and exposed the value of these relationships.

This is a powerful dynamic that is sadly lacking in todays fast-paced, spread-out society. As we journey through life, numerous meaningful relationships are established. Sharing those relationships adds tremendous value and, as stated in the previous chapter, one of the best things we can give to others is the meaningful relationships we have formed.

Forms 32 – 34

The first sets of forms for you to fill out in this chapter are designed to help you identify the wise counselors that you have in your life. There will also be times when insight, experience and words of wisdom will be needed by your spouse or your family regarding some of life's decisions. These may include such areas as strategic planning, priority sorting, judgment calls, relationship issues, conflict dynamics, business and investment decisions, financial considerations and general advice. Those who currently are in your inner circle are there for a reason. As you identify and list these individuals, include specific areas of strength for each. This will be very helpful for those you share this information with.

Why do so many people make important decisions without consulting the advice of wise people? It may involve pride, but more than likely it is because most haven't taken the time to establish relationships with or clearly identify who the men or women of wisdom are in their life. Before moving forward, take the necessary time and bring to completion the list of wise counselors in your life that your family can rely on, now and in the future.

If you do not currently have a mentor or cannot quickly come up with a list of wise counselors in your life; I challenge you to seek them out. These are probably the busiest, most involved people you will meet. They are not standing around waiting to find you, you must find them and when you do, ask to get together. Offer to buy them breakfast. Let them know that you have some specific things about which you would appreciate their insight. They typically don't waste time, but they do invest time. Take the initiative and show yourself worthy of that investment. These relationships are hard to find, but because of the nature and depth of the conversations, they can develop very quickly. Birds of a feather do flock together. As you begin this journey, this person of wisdom will introduce you to others. Over time, your insights will grow. Before you know it, someone will be asking to meet with you.

Forms 35 – 45

Wisdom involves the proper application of knowledge. We know that death is an inevitable part of life. We know that preparing for death on a number of different levels is wise. Properly projecting future financial needs and developing a well thought-out insurance strategy are important parts of our planning.

The next step in this chapter involves documenting the insurance coverage you have and the related monies your beneficiaries will receive. In addition you will be outlining such things as social security benefits, retirement income and inheritance.

So, what about insurance?

I wonder if there were insurance companies and insurance salesmen during Moses' time. Let's just say for a minute that there were. What type of marketing plan and advertising budget would they have put together? Who would have been their spokesperson? What would just the right person have been worth? If Tiger Woods received $122 million for smiling in front of a Buick, think of what Moses would have gotten from "Promised Land Mutual" for signing off on quotes like:

- "God turns men back to dust saying, "Return to dust, O sons of men"

- "God sweeps men away in the sleep of death; they are like the new grass of the morning."

- "All our days pass away…"

This is the leader of the nation talking. The marketing team would be doing back flips. Forget what it may cost, quadruple the size of the sales force and sponsor the chariot races with bigger-than-life Moses banners. Flood the landscape with these quotes and sell everyone on investing in a universal life policy. It's the biggest no-brainer in the history of man.

Moses held his expiration date in plain view. As he observed the brevity of men's days he connected them, not to life insurance, but to the presence of a living and eternal God. One of the objectives of Unfinished Business is to help you examine your life and your affairs in light of God's perspective. This is challenging. This does not come easily or naturally for any of us. If you don't slow down, gaining that perspective doesn't stand a chance.

Walt Henrichsen writes:

> "Your sense of mortality determines your view of reality. To the degree that you understand the brevity of your life you will seek to avoid what one person called 'the tyranny of the urgent,' giving yourself instead to those opportunities that best define your purpose. You of course do not know how many days you have on earth, but if you apply your heart to the wisdom of God, that will not matter, for the Lord will not evaluate your life on the basis of what you produce. Rather, He will judge you based on the degree to which you lived your life sharing His values. If you accept His values as your own, you have no time to waste on those ingredients the world says are the measures of success."
>
> (DIARY OF A DESPERATE MAN, DAY 353)

Temporal and immediate things are easy to grasp. We can touch today. The affairs of today are much easier to grasp than anything in eternity. I can give priority to what I know is going to happen in the next 24 hours or later this week. Investing thought and energy and resources into eternity or what seems like the distant future, well, that requires a different mindset. Obtaining that perspective requires us to slow down and be still before our God. When we do this, we can examine our affairs in a whole new light.

How does insurance fit in?

Karle is a friend of mine. He has been a member of our IRON group. He was part of this project way back when we called it "Readiness." Karle sells life insurance. Talk about owning a lemonade stand on the hottest day of the year. The timing for what he does couldn't have been better, right? I mean, in light of this project, all of the IRON guys were lined up to review insurance needs, right?

Not so right. Case in point: during the process of putting our affairs in order, we updated a number of things. One of these was analyzing our insurance coverage. I love Karle, but reviewing insurance needs was painful. What type of insurance is most prudent? How much is enough? What does overkill look like? What do we really need to cover? How much is this going to cost? You want me to buy a policy to place in a trust to cover the inheritance tax so my family doesn't lose the stuff I leave?!! Give me a break! I put off the final meeting with Karle for months. Getting my teeth cleaned was a higher priority and I viewed it as more enjoyable.

I sought wise counsel from several key advisers. Sandy and I discussed, at length, our projected needs and compared that to the options and choices in front of us. Finally, we decided on what would best fit our needs. When Karle and I finally got together, he said something very interesting: "When I'm selling insurance, no one is happy to see me. At the funeral, everyone is happy to see me." I can tell you, I get that.

We do not position ourselves as advisors or experts when it comes to life insurance; nor do we enter this discussion with any agenda or bias. Our challenge to you is to take time in your life to be still before God and seek to live in such a way that what you do inside your days is important in His eyes.

When it comes to insurance, identify your needs and research your options. We have included some very basic guidelines. Your accountant, attorney and a trusted insurance broker should collaborate to lay out options that would be best for your family. Once these decisions are made and the policies are acquired, be sure to keep the original copies in a safe place. A home safe or safety deposit box is recommended. In addition, record the policy information utilizing the forms provided, and file these pages in your Important Documents file.

This is one of the three items that most commonly is left as unfinished business. I encourage you to establish a deadline for completing this part of putting your affairs in order. Have someone with a military mindset hold you accountable.

Also, keep in mind that as time goes on, your needs may change. Sandy and I plan to review this every 5 years. I anticipate that we are at a place now where the need for change would be small or non-existent. During these first 33 years of our marriage, our personal circumstances have changed quite a bit. During this time we have made changes to our coverage four times.

What about disability?

Man is frail. Often that frailty can lead to disability. This is something few healthy people want to think about, yet it is a documented statistic: in their lifetime, nearly 30% of Americans become disabled either cognitively or in mobility, eyesight and hearing.

It can hit home suddenly!

I remember specific parts of a particular day very clearly. It was early autumn of my sophomore year in high school. I arrived home around 4 PM and my mother was sitting at the corner desk in our dining room, humped over and talking on the phone. She was crying. I stopped in my tracks and just stared at her. She looked up and said: "Your father has been hurt…. badly; I have to go to the hospital." I told her I would go with her. This is where my memory blurs. I don't know how we got there. We only had one car. My dad worked for a commercial construction company with projects throughout southeastern Wisconsin and he always took the car. I'm guessing Aunt Marlene picked us up.

As we rushed into the emergency room, I caught a glimpse of my father being pushed down the hallway on a stretcher with what seemed to be a doctor, two nurses and another guy working on him as they walked. My mother was able to catch up to the convoy and they paused long enough for her to hold my dad's hand and get a quick update. As she returned to me, wiping away tears, she explained that they were cutting off his pants and his boots and were taking him in for emergency surgery. He had been working on some scaffolding and had fallen off. The good news was he fell straight down, feet first. If he had fallen any other way it would have been much more critical and probably fatal. The bad news was both feet and ankles were messed up pretty badly.

My father spent most of the next 18 months in the hospital. He went through multiple surgeries and excruciating rehabilitation. He was never able to return to full-time work of any kind. Disability carries a tough blow to established routines. As a witness to my dad's inner strength and character, he has made the most of it. Today, at age 78, he still does part-time deliveries for my brother's sporting goods store. Customers nicknamed him "Fast Eddie." Initially, I thought it was in response to my dad's great sense of humor. If you have a weakness, he'll expose it, assign a nick-name and get you to laugh at yourself. Because of the injury, my dad walks with the same speed you and I would have if we were wearing concrete boots, so the name sounded like appropriate pay-back. My brother is convinced it has a whole lot more to do with his ability to interrupt an owner in an important meeting, get paid the C.O.D., and move on. I guess you can do that when you're wearing a 20-pound boot.

My dad and mom could be the poster couple for working through disability. At the time of the accident all six kids were still at home. We all pulled together and, though finances were very tight, and despite the fact it was extremely hard to see my dad go through the pain and transition, I can say I have no memory of feeling short-changed or wanting for anything. A different set of priorities took precedent.

Is there anything I should do today to prepare for possible disability?
Form 46

There are a number of legislative changes and enhancements that our Federal Government has introduced in recent years to help those with disability. These include the Disability Act, The Disability Discrimination Act and The Disability Living Allowance. Should the need arise; we suggest you explore all available options. There are literally hundreds of web-sites on the internet with information that can help lead you in the right direction.

Following is a list of some key documents we recommend you fill out now, and keep clearly indexed in your Important Documents file in the event that you become cognitively disabled sometime in the future.

- Power of Attorney for Assets
- Power of Attorney for Medical Decisions
- Guardian over my Property
- Guardian over my Person
- Living Will

Aside from the potential help that may be available from the federal government, it will be helpful to identify the sources and amount of income that you currently have in place should you or your spouse become disabled.

What is a Living Will?
Form 47

A Living Will is a document which states whether you wish be kept on artificial life support. This document may also appoint someone to make health-care decisions on your behalf, in case you are unable to do so.

Note: For liability reasons we have not included a form for doing this. We recommend you seek legal advice relating to the specific requirements in your state, or you can go to a local bookstore or online and purchase the necessary forms.

What about a Living Trust?

This will be addressed along with your Will in Chapter 6. A Living Trust is a tool that some use to avoid probate. Probate is the legal process that inventories and distributes a person's property after death. Many people aim to avoid probate because it can be time consuming and expensive. A Living

Trust allows for the transfer of assets, free of probate, within weeks prior to death. This along with other items relating to the distribution of possessions will be addressed in the next chapter.

Estimated Future Budget

In case you haven't figured it out, Chapter 5 leads the league in most forms to fill out. Hang in there and don't get sloppy. All of this stuff is important for those we leave behind. . We will soon be transitioning to more enjoyable things like who you are, your values and your hope. Meanwhile don't lose focus and don't allow yourself to get distracted. Remember the "pep-talk" about giving this your BEST effort? Now would be a good time to replay that tape. Think of this as the start of the fourth quarter. Do you know how many games are lost in the last quarter because of fatigue? What's that? You're a baseball fan? Ok, look at this as the bottom of the seventh and there is no bull pen. You are on the mound and it's all about your ability to dig deep and take your team to closure. Whatever motivates you, now is the time. Hug your wife, call your kids, do some arm curls while looking in the mirror…do whatever it takes.

This is where most guys drop off. Don't let it happen to you. If it helps, imagine your family finding this book unfinished after you are gone. This is not the time to lay down.

Still waffling? Try this. Give your self an award….. No, not now, when you are done. That's right. What would you like? That's too big! Reload. Pick something kind of small, but nice. Something you'd really like as a gift, but you just don't feel right buying for yourself. This is a lot of work. It's easy to be unorganized. Finishing business is tough stuff. So, reward yourself. Recommit to giving this your BEST effort and finishing all the forms in all the chapters.

Form 48

OK…one more form to fill out before we move on to Chapter 6. Form 48 is the Estimated Future Budget form. The Current Budget Form you filled out in Chapter 3 relates to today's income, today's finances and today's needs. The Future Budget Form will help you determine today if you currently have enough support to meet the estimated future needs of your spouse and family.

Most of the forms in Chapter 6 will help you identify all the pieces you currently have in place. We recommend that you seek practical and wise counsel as you review your affairs and put these things in order. These are all very key to the options your family will or will not have in years ahead. Apply knowledge. Exercise wisdom. That wisdom will be caught by those you care for the most.

Wise Counsel

Updated: _____

LAWYER	
Name:	
Name of Firm:	
Street Address:	
City, State, Zip:	
Home Phone:	
Cell:	
Office:	
Email Address:	
Areas of Strength:	

ACCOUNTANT	
Name:	
Name of Firm:	
Street Address:	
City, State, Zip:	
Home Phone:	
Cell:	
Office:	
Email Address:	
Areas of Strength:	

Wise Counsel

FORM 33

Updated: _____

PERSONAL ADVISOR / MENTOR
Name:
Street Address:
City, State, Zip:
Home Phone:
Cell:
Office:
Email Address:
Areas of Strength:

PERSONAL ADVISOR / MENTOR
Name:
Street Address:
City, State, Zip:
Home Phone:
Cell:
Office:
Email Address:
Areas of Strength:

Wise Counsel

FORM 34

Updated: _____

PERSONAL ADVISOR / MENTOR	
Name:	
Street Address:	
City, State, Zip:	
Home Phone:	
Cell:	
Office:	
Email Address:	
Areas of Strength:	

PERSONAL ADVISOR / MENTOR	
Name:	
Street Address:	
City, State, Zip:	
Home Phone:	
Cell:	
Office:	
Email Address:	
Areas of Strength:	

What Type of Insurance Should I Have and How Much Coverage is Necessary?

Updated: _____

A common gauge that many use during the prime years of growing a family is 10 times annual earnings. With proper investing and debt reduction, this ratio typically reduces in later years. (Second to die, estate tax coverage not included.) A combination of term-and full-life coverage can blend nicely to cover the needs in each stage of life.

An alternate approach which is recommended by many accountants and financial planners includes the following:

a. First, focus on needs. What obligations remain if you should die prematurely?

   i. Providing for your spouse

   ii. Providing for the children until age 18

   iii. Providing for children's education

   iv. Paying off mortgage and other debts

b. Second, focus on resources. What assets will be available?

   i. Savings

   ii. Retirement assets

   iii. Company Life insurance

   iv. Social Security

c. The gap between needs and resources can be filled with life insurance. Each year, needs should diminish and resources should grow and the need for life insurance should shrink.

Working through the financial projections and worksheets in this book should help you identify more clearly what your family's needs may be.

Our advice is to find trustworthy legal and professional counsel to help identify what would be in your family's best interests.

Insurance Inventory

FORM 36

Updated: _____

LIFE INSURANCE

Insurance Company: _____ Insured: _____
Agent: _____ Phone: _____
Address: _____
Beneficiary: _____ Policy #: _____
Premium Due Date: _____ Premium Payments: _____
Value: _____ Face Amount: _____ Cash Value: _____
Original Document Location: _____

LIFE INSURANCE

Insurance Company: _____ Insured: _____
Agent: _____ Phone: _____
Address: _____
Beneficiary: _____ Policy #: _____
Premium Due Date: _____ Premium Payments: _____
Value: _____ Face Amount: _____ Cash Value: _____
Original Document Location: _____

LIFE INSURANCE

Insurance Company: _____ Insured: _____
Agent: _____ Phone: _____
Address: _____
Beneficiary: _____ Policy #: _____
Premium Due Date: _____ Premium Payments: _____
Value: _____ Face Amount: _____ Cash Value: _____
Original Document Location: _____

LIFE INSURANCE

Insurance Company: _____ Insured: _____
Agent: _____ Phone: _____
Address: _____
Beneficiary: _____ Policy #: _____
Premium Due Date: _____ Premium Payments: _____
Value: _____ Face Amount: _____ Cash Value: _____
Original Document Location: _____

Insurance Inventory (continued)

FORM 37

Updated: _____

Homeowner's (Tenant's) Insurance

Insurance Company: _____
Agent: _____ Phone: _____
Address: _____
Property Covered: _____ Policy #: _____
Coverage: _____
Premium Due Date: _____ Premium Payment: _____
Original Document Location: _____

Automobile Insurance

Insurance Company: _____
Agent: _____ Phone: _____
Address: _____
Vehicle Covered: _____ Policy #: _____
Coverage: _____
Premium Due Date: _____ Premium Payment: _____
Original Document Location: _____

Insurance Company: _____
Agent: _____ Phone: _____
Address: _____
Vehicle Covered: _____ Policy #: _____
Coverage: _____
Premium Due Date: _____ Premium Payment: _____
Original Document Location: _____

Liability Insurance

Insurance Company: _____
Agent: _____ Phone: _____
Address: _____
Person Covered: _____ Policy #: _____
Coverage: _____
Premium Due Date: _____ Premium Payment: _____
Original Document Location: _____

Insurance Inventory (continued)

FORM 38

Updated: _____

HEALTH INSURANCE

Insurance Company:		Insured:	
Agent:		Phone:	
Address:			
Person(s) Covered:		Policy #:	
Coverage:			
Premium Due Date:		Premium Payment:	
Original Document Location:			

DISABILITY INSURANCE

Insurance Company:		Insured:	
Agent:		Phone:	
Address:			
Person(s) Covered:		Policy #:	
Coverage:			
Premium Due Date:		Premium Payment:	
Original Document Location:			

OTHER INSURANCE

Insurance Company:		Insured:	
Agent:		Phone:	
Address:			
Person(s) Covered:		Policy #:	
Coverage:			
Premium Due Date:		Premium Payment:	
Original Document Location:			

OTHER INSURANCE

Insurance Company:		Insured:	
Agent:		Phone:	
Address:			
Person(s) Covered:		Policy #:	
Coverage:			
Premium Due Date:		Premium Payment:	
Original Document Location:			

Work-Related Insurance

(Attach copy of Summary of Benefits from policy / employee handbook)

FORM 39

Updated: _____

Employer Name: _____
Address: _____
Phone: _____
Fax: _____
Person to Contact: _____

Life Insurance Company: _____
Address: _____
Phone: _____
Fax: _____
Dollar Amount: _____
Accidental Death Amt: _____
Person to Contact: _____
Policy #: _____
Original Document Location: _____

Health Insurance Company: _____
Address: _____
Phone: _____
Fax: _____
Person to Contact: _____
Policy #: _____
Summary of Policy: _____
Original Document Location: _____

Disability Insurance Company: _____
Address: _____
Phone: _____
Fax: _____
Person to Contact: _____
Policy #: _____
Summary of Policy: _____
Original Document Location: _____

Work-Related Insurance (continued)

FORM 40

Updated: _____

Dental Insurance Company: _____

Address: _____
Phone: _____
Fax: _____

Person to Contact: _____
Policy #: _____

Summary of Policy: _____

Original Document Location: _____

Cancer Insurance Company: _____

Address: _____
Phone: _____
Fax: _____

Person to Contact: _____
Policy #: _____

Summary of Policy: _____

Original Document Location: _____

Other Insurance Company: _____

Address: _____
Phone: _____
Fax: _____

Person to Contact: _____
Policy #: _____

Summary of Policy: _____

Original Document Location: _____

Social Security

FORM 41

Updated: _____

Family Member	Name on Card	Social Security Number
Head of Household:		
Spouse:		
Other:		
Other:		
Other:		
Other:		
Other:		

Other Information

Location of Cards: _____
Address of nearest Social Security Office: _____
Soc. Security Phone: _____

Benefit Information / Description

_____
_____
_____
_____
_____

How to Determine Your Social Security Benefits

Facts about your Social Security benefits may be obtained by calling the Social Security office toll-free at 1-800-772-1213. If you are age 60 or older, you may obtain a benefits estimate by phone. If you are under 60, you must request a form, which you will complete and mail back to the Social Security office. Provide your full name, your social security number and street address. Your earnings record will be sent along with other information about your possible benefits at various ages. Telephone numbers and Social Security regulations are subject to change. Please check your local telephone directory if the toll-free number noted above is not in service. Please note that you can now obtain this information on the web at www.saa.gov.

How to File for Social Security Benefits upon Death of a Spouse

To receive Social Security benefits, go in person to the Social Security office as soon as possible after your spouse's death. A delay may void some of the benefits. When you go, take your spouse's social security card and death certificate. Also take your birth certificate, marriage certificate and birth certificates for each child.

Company Retirement Benefits

FORM 42

Updated: _____

COMPANY INFORMATION	
Name:	
Address:	
City, State, Zip:	
Phone:	
Fax:	
Person to Contact:	

BENEFIT INFORMATION	
Brief Description of Plan:	
Monthly amount paid to Beneficiary(s) at death, if any:	
Lump sum amount paid to Beneficiary(s) at death, if any:	
Latest Value of Plan:	Date:
Documentation Location:	

Estimate of Retirement Income

(Update annually)

FORM 43

Updated: _____

Source of Income	Amount of Monthly Income
Social Security:	
Salary (Part-time / Full-time):	
Savings:	
Investments:	
Real Estate:	
Business Income:	
Veterans Benefits:	
Company Retirement Benefits:	
Other:	
Other:	
Other:	
Other:	
TOTAL MONTHLY INCOME:	$

Future Income upon Loss of a Spouse

FORM 44

(Contact your accountant or financial planner to confirm the impact taxes will have on your income)

Updated: _____

Following the loss of _____
the estimated monthly income for our family will be as follows:

Source of Income	Amount of Monthly Income
Survivor's Employment Earnings:	
Social Security:	
Company Retirement Benefits:	
Investments / Interest:	
Savings / Interest:	
Life Insurance Proceeds / Interest:	
Real Estate Income:	
Other:	
Other:	
Other:	
Other:	
TOTAL MONTHLY INCOME:	$
LESS Monthly Spending:	$
SURPLUS or DEFICIT:	$
TOTAL LIQUID CASH AVAILABLE:	$

Inheritance Information

FORM 45

Updated: _____

I may receive an inheritance from: _____

The amount of the inheritance may be as much as $ _____

Upon my death, my heirs [○ WILL] [○ WILL NOT] receive a distribution or benefits from a trust.

If yes, the instrument was created by: _____

The Trust instrument can be found: _____

I [○ AM] [○ AM NOT] currently the Trustee for a trust.

If I am a Trustee, the trust document is located: _____

I [○ AM] [○ AM NOT] a beneficiary of a trust.

If I am a beneficiary, the trust document is located: _____

I am currently Legal Guardian for the following person(s):

_____

_____

_____

Documents appointing me are located: _____

(140)

In the Event of My Incapacity

FORM 46

Updated: _____

I have appointed the following persons to act on my behalf if I become disabled:

Power of Attorney over my Assets: 1st _____

2nd _____

Power of Attorney for Medical Decisions: 1st _____

2nd _____

Guardian over my Property: 1st _____

2nd _____

Guardian over my Person: 1st _____

2nd _____

It is my desire that the persons having the above powers of attorney act on my behalf rather than a guardian being appointed, unless my family believes guardianship is necessary.

In the event of my incapacity, I [○ DO] [○ DO NOT] want to be kept at home as long as possible, taking into account the cost.

In the event of my incapacity, the following is additional information which I think is important for my family and advisors to know:

_____

_____

_____

_____

_____

_____

(141)

Living Will

THIS SHEET SERVES AS A REMINDER TO FILE A COPY OF YOUR LIVING WILL IN YOUR KEY DOCUMENTS FILE.

We have not included a form, but recommend seeking legal advice relating to the specific requirements in your state. You can also go to a local bookstore or online and purchase the applicable forms.

Estimated Future Budget

(Update annually)

FORM 48

Updated: _____

	GROSS MONTHLY INCOME:	$
	Salary:	
	Interest:	
	Dividends:	
	Other:	
	Other:	

Less

1	Charitable Giving:	
2	Federal Tax:	
	State Tax:	
	FICA:	

	NET SPENDABLE INCOME:	$

3	HOUSING:	$
	Mortgage (or rent):	
	Insurance:	
	Taxes:	
	Electricity:	
	Gas:	
	Water:	
	Sanitation:	
	Telephone:	
	Maintenance:	
	Other:	
	Other:	

4	FOOD / GROCERIES:	$
5	AUTOMOBILE:	$
	Payments:	
	Gas / Oil:	
	Insurance:	
	License / Taxes:	
	Maintenance / Repair:	

6	INSURANCE:	$
	Life:	
	Medical:	
	Other:	

7	DEBTS:	$
	Credit Card:	
	Loans / Notes:	
	Other:	
	Other:	

8	RECREATION:	$
	Eating Out:	
	Memberships:	
	Activities:	
	Vacation:	
	Hobbies:	
	Other:	

9	CLOTHING:	$
10	SAVINGS:	$
	Personal:	
	Educational:	
	Retirement:	

11	MEDICAL:	$
	Doctor(s):	
	Dentist:	
	Rx Drugs:	
	Other:	

12	MISCELLANEOUS:	$
	Cable / Internet:	
	Toiletries, Cosmetics:	
	Beauty Shop / Barber:	
	Laundry / Dry-cleaning:	
	Allowances, Lunches:	
	Subscriptions:	
	Gifts (inc. Christmas):	
	Decorating:	
	Other:	
	Other:	

13	INVESTMENTS:	$
14	SCHOOL / CHILD CARE:	$
	Tuition:	
	Supplies:	
	Clothing:	
	Transportation:	
	Day Care:	
	Other:	

	TOTAL EXPENSES:	$

INCOME VERSUS EXPENSES

	Net Spendable Income:	
	Less Expenses:	
	UNALLOCATED SURPLUS:	$

(145)

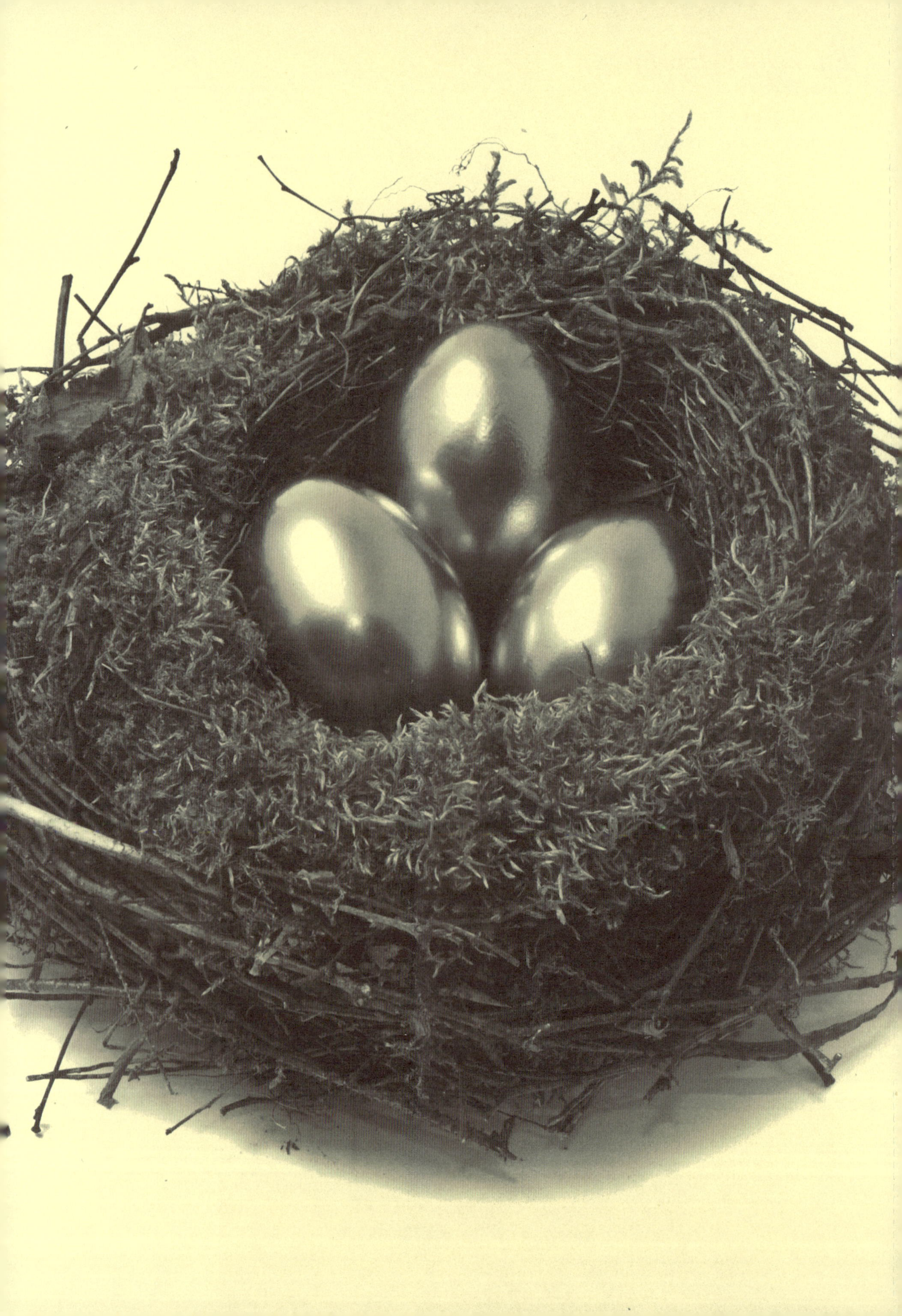

CHAPTER 6

From *Wisdom* to *Value*

PUTTING CLOSURE TO STUFF

The very mention of estate planning and preparing a will suggests time, difficult planning and a whole lot of work. Most people procrastinate in this area. Few embrace it. Why is that? If you have procrastinated in putting your affairs in order, specifically preparing your estate documents, what is the underlying reason? Procrastination leaves clues...

Many studies have been done and much has been written on the causes of procrastination. Fear has been identified as a leading factor. Fear of failure... Fear of an unpleasant experience... Fear of doing it wrong... I was taught that F.E.A.R. is an acronym for False Evidence Appearing Real. Most fears are imaginary and, in this case, probably not the main motivation for procrastination.

Below are some additional key reasons why people procrastinate:

1. **Complexity.** Some projects can seem daunting and cause many people to procrastinate. When one is overwhelmed, it helps to break a project down into smaller components and tackle each part individually. There may be some application here.

2. **No appeal.** Most people will tackle a project they enjoy, but will continually delay working on tasks that are less appealing. We will discuss this in more detail in a few moments. This book has been all about shifting perspective from temporal to eternal. Applying that shift to all the documents associated with your estate may have a huge impact on your appeal to address it. In Chapter 4 I suggested implementing a reward system for the completion of this project. If you add to that a change in perspective, procrastination will fade.

3. **Prioritizing.** There are more options than time in our lives. Failing to plan and failing to prioritize will leave important items left undone as we react to the urgent or to what brings pleasure. Failure to see the pleasure in estate planning keeps it on the shelf for many, and forever left undone.

4. **Distractions** are a major cause of procrastination. It takes a high level of discipline and determination to stay focused and bring to completion complex tasks like this. Time is a valuable commodity. Guard your time and attention in order to apply everything needed to bring all the pieces to completion. Avoid allowing some of these very important legal documents to be missing from your files, rendering much of this work void.

When we understand why we procrastinate, we will be able to implement strategies to put an end to our procrastination.

If you have procrastinated in putting your affairs in order, it may be because of one of the causes listed above or it may be because of a disconnection in understanding for which age all of the work of our hands is deployed; this age or the one to come. I will procrastinate indefinitely; when futile work is required that lacks value or meaning. I am drawn and inspired to tackle work impacting family, friends and people I love.

Joseph's listing in God's "Hall of Fame" in Hebrews 11 is as amazing as it is inspiring. Amazing because of the reason…instructions concerning his bones. Inspiring because of the perspective Joseph had beyond his current circumstances as Egypt's number two man. If you were in Joseph's shoes, would you have chosen to be buried in the Pyramids, assuring fame and legacy for untold generations? Or would you have given instructions in the direction of your hope, and the relationship you have with the one true God?

In this chapter, you will give instructions concerning your bones. Take your time. Get input. Strategize. Personalize this. Be deliberate. Make this a work that you are motivated by and excited about. Ensure that your wishes reflect your life, your values and your hope.

It is highly advisable that you involve legal counsel in the finalization of your estate documents. We have included an estate document checklist to help organize your efforts. Please keep in mind that the definitions provided are for general education, not legal advice.

Form 49
Will

A will is a document which states what individuals want done to their property when they die, and how they want that property distributed. It specifically identifies what property should go to which people. To ensure that a will is legally valid, the person preparing it must follow various formalities and legal requirements.

Living Will

A living will is a legal document making known one's wishes regarding life-prolonging medical treatments. It can also be referred to as an advance directive, health care directive, or a physician's directive.

Living Trust

A living trust is a mechanism for holding and distributing a person's assets to avoid probate. This was discussed in Chapter 4. We recommend that you discuss this option with a trusted attorney.

Insurance Trust

A life insurance trust is a trust that is set up for the purpose of owning a life insurance policy. If the insured is the owner of the policy, the proceeds of the policy will be subject to estate tax when he dies. But if he transfers ownership to a life insurance trust, the proceeds will be completely free of estate tax. (The proceeds will be exempt from income tax either way.)

Given the current estate tax rate of 45%, a life insurance trust can save hundreds of thousands of dollars in estate taxes. However, there are several drawbacks to such an arrangement:

1. You can't change the beneficiary of the policy.

2. You can't borrow from the policy.

3. You can't transfer an existing policy to the trust—unless you live for at least three more years.

4. The life insurance trust must be irrevocable.

5. Premium payments may use up your estate tax exemption.

6. You must assign a trustee.

Charitable Trust

Charitable trusts are a frequently used, but rarely understood planning tool. They can provide financial benefit to you, as a donor, while allowing you to leave more than you might otherwise bequeath to the charities of your choice. Charitable Remainder Trusts can be an attractive way to reposition appreciated assets such as real estate into a portfolio of stocks and bonds while minimizing the tax implications they would normally face.

A Charitable Remainder Trust is an instrument that pays income to a specified person or persons for a set period of time and then delivers the remaining principal to one or more charities upon termination of the trust. In a typical example, a donor will contribute appreciated assets to the trust (which generates an income tax deduction). The donor then receives an income stream for the rest of his/her life (and the spouse's life, if applicable), and instructs that upon their death, the remaining assets in the trust be given to a charity or to the donor's private foundation.

Minor's Trust

The Minor's Trust 2503 (c) is a trust whereby assets are managed until a child or grandchild reaches a specified age. Upon reaching the specified age, the child has full use and control over the assets. The person setting up the trust cannot receive any income from the assets held in the trust. All undistributed income is taxed at trust rates, which are moderate. The person setting up the trust is able to control the time at which the minor has access to the assets given.

General Power of Attorney

A power of attorney is a document that allows you to appoint a person or organization to handle your affairs while you're unavailable or unable to do so. The person or organization you appoint is referred to as an "Attorney-in-Fact" or "Agent."

General Power of Attorney – (Also called a Limited PofA) authorizes your Agent to act on your behalf in a variety of different situations.

Special Power of Attorney – authorizes your Agent to act on your behalf in specific situations only.

Health Care Power of Attorney – allows you to appoint someone to make health care decisions for you if you're incapacitated.

"Durable" Power of Attorney – The general, special and health care powers of attorney can all be made "durable" by adding certain text to the document. This means that the document will remain in effect or take effect if you become mentally incompetent.

Revocation of Power of Attorney –- allows you to revoke a power of attorney document.

A General Power of Attorney is very broad and provides extensive powers to the person or organization appointed by you as your agent. These powers usually include:

- Handling banking transactions
- Entering safety deposit boxes
- Handling transactions involving U.S. securities
- Buying and selling property
- Purchasing life insurance
- Settling claims
- Entering into contracts
- Exercising stock rights
- Buying, managing or selling real estate
- Filing tax returns
- Handling matters related to government benefits

You also have the option to grant the following additional powers to your agent:

- Maintaining and operating business interests
- Employing professional assistance
- Making gifts
- Making transfers to revocable ("living") trusts
- Disclaiming interests (this has to do with estate planning strategies to avoid estate taxes)

A general power of attorney is usually used to allow your agent to handle all of your affairs during a period of time when you are unable to do so. For example, when you are traveling out of the state or country or when you are physically or mentally unable to handle your affairs. A general power of attorney is frequently included as part of an estate plan to assure that you are covered in the possibility that you need someone to handle your financial affairs because you are unable to do so.

Again, this information is given for educational purposes and is not intended to serve as legal advice. A trusted attorney, insurance broker and financial planner will serve you well in these areas.

(151)

Distribution of Possessions
Forms 50 – 52

Many families have been torn apart over the distribution of possessions after mom and dad die. One day siblings are grieving over the loss, the next day they are fighting over who gets various items around the house. The Distribution of Possessions form has been included to help avoid that devastating scenario, but also to allow you to choose to whom you would like to give certain collectibles, jewelry, books and memorabilia. It is common for these to extend beyond your immediate family.

Most of these items will not be specifically mentioned in your Will. This would not be practical due to the addition of new items and length of the list. The fact that this list would probably need to be updated more regularly than the other main components of your Last Will would mean adding unnecessary cost and complexity. Keeping it separate can simplify this portion.

Continued Giving Plan
Form 53

This form allows you to identify specific charitable contributions that you have been making and wish to continue making after your death. While the Charitable Trust allows you to leave larger assets to charities of your choice or a foundation, this form is intended to express your desire for on-going financial support to organizations whose mission and purpose you believe in.

Funeral Instructions
Forms 54 - 57

In my home study on the third shelf up, just left of the fireplace I display a lynch pin. I purchased it four years ago, shortly after Gayle Jackson wished me a Happy "Lynch Pin" Sunday. I didn't immediately catch the meaning. The look on my face must have given it away. As I stood there sporting the bright new tie I had bought in celebration of Easter, Gayle smiled and said, "Lynch Pin, that's what Easter is. Pull out Jesus' resurrection and everything about Christianity falls apart. His redemptive death and Resurrection is the lynch pin of our faith." Our guilt is imputed to Christ on the cross and His redeeming punishment is imputed to us. Jesus paid the price and conquered death. He rose as the first fruit. As a result we can approach God, seek forgiveness and be totally cleansed. This is God's redemptive plan. This is what God's calls us to respond to. This is the lynch pin of our faith.

For Christians, death is real, but it is also temporal. Beyond death lies our hope of resurrection to a life that is both dynamic and eternal in the visible presence of our God. It is this Resurrection faith which enables Christians to contemplate our unavoidable departure from this life without fear. This is the dynamic behind funerals in which a spirit of celebration and hope actually trumps loss. I have attended funerals in which attendees are so drawn to this message of hope, forgiveness and salvation that they turn from chasing happiness and fulfillment in the temporal to finding eternal perspective.

Moses documents how short our days are on earth. Joseph sets an example for all time of connecting our bones with our hope. As you prepare specific instructions concerning your bones and the funeral that surrounds them, I encourage you to think through all the aspects of those few days immediately after your death.. As you begin to document your plans, discuss them with others who share your values and faith. Get their input. Those who attend my funeral will be handed a lynch pin as they enter a time of celebration. This is an unusual topic to network over, but remember how Moses held his expiration in plain view. Generally speaking, your Will is not read until after the funeral. What everyone experienced at your funeral should be a seamless connection to what is written in your Will, Trusts and Distribution of Possessions documents.

The decisions you make surrounding these documents and the days surrounding your death can have tremendous impact on those who attend your funeral and generational impact on your immediate family.

We will continue personalizing this process in Chapter 7.

Estate Documents Checklist

FORM 49

Updated: _____

WILL ○ *Current* ○ *Needs revision* ○ *Need, but do not have*
Persons covered: _____
Location: _____
Who to Call: _____

LIVING WILL ○ *Current* ○ *Needs revision* ○ *Need, but do not have*
Persons covered: _____
Location: _____
Who to Call: _____

LIVING TRUST ○ *Current* ○ *Needs revision* ○ *Need, but do not have*
Persons covered: _____
Location: _____
Who to Call: _____

INSURANCE TRUST ○ *Current* ○ *Needs revision* ○ *Need, but do not have*
Persons covered: _____
Location: _____
Who to Call: _____

CHARITABLE TRUST ○ *Current* ○ *Needs revision* ○ *Need, but do not have*
Persons covered: _____
Location: _____
Who to Call: _____

MINOR'S TRUST ○ *Current* ○ *Needs revision* ○ *Need, but do not have*
Persons covered: _____
Location: _____
Who to Call: _____

GENERAL POWER OF ATTORNEY ○ *Current* ○ *Needs revision* ○ *Need, but do not have*
Persons covered: _____
Location: _____
Who to Call: _____

MEDICAL POWER OF ATTORNEY ○ *Current* ○ *Needs revision* ○ *Need, but do not have*
Persons covered: _____
Location: _____
Who to Call: _____

MEDICAL DIRECTIVE ○ *Current* ○ *Needs revision* ○ *Need, but do not have*
Persons covered: _____
Location: _____
Who to Call: _____

Distribution of Possessions

FORM 50

Updated: _____

Regarding certain items that are not specifically covered in the will, the following is my desire relating to the distribution of possessions.

ITEM	GIFTED TO
JEWELRY	
COLLECTIBLES	
APPAREL	
BOOKS	

Distribution of Possessions (continued)

FORM 51

Updated: _____

ITEM	GIFTED TO
MEMORABILIA	
FURNISHINGS	
TOOLS	
ELECTRONICS	

(159)

Distribution of Possessions (continued)

FORM 52

Updated: _____

ITEM	GIFTED TO
VEHICLES	
ART	
MEMBERSHIP	
MISCELLANEOUS	

(161)

Continued Giving Plan

FORM 53

Updated: _____

Following are charities or ministries that have been supported and I would like to continue contributions to them as long as both the need and means exist.

Name of Organization:	
Address:	
City, State, Zip Code:	
Phone:	
Contact Name:	
Historical Contribution:	
Recommended Forward Contribution:	

Name of Organization:	
Address:	
City, State, Zip Code:	
Phone:	
Contact Name:	
Historical Contribution:	
Recommended Forward Contribution:	

Name of Organization:	
Address:	
City, State, Zip Code:	
Phone:	
Contact Name:	
Historical Contribution:	
Recommended Forward Contribution:	

Name of Organization:	
Address:	
City, State, Zip Code:	
Phone:	
Contact Name:	
Historical Contribution:	
Recommended Forward Contribution:	

Funeral Instructions

FORM 54

Updated: _____

Funeral Home Preference:	
Address:	Phone:
	Fax:
Person to Contact:	
Description of any arrangements already made:	

Viewing Wishes:	❍ *Open Casket* ❍ *Closed Casket*
Location of Service:	❍ *Church* ❍ *Funeral Home*
Name of Church/Funeral Home:	
Address:	Phone:
	Contact:

REQUESTS FOR FUNERAL SERVICE

Name of Minister:	Phone:
Description of Service:	
Musical Selections:	
	Organist: ❍*Y* ❍*N* Pianist: ❍*Y* ❍*N* Vocalist: ❍*Y* ❍*N*
Special Requests (Biblical Passages, clothing, etc.):	

Funeral Instructions (continued)

FORM 55

Updated: _____

Name of Cemetery:	
Address:	Phone:
	Fax:
Location of Cemetery Lot(s):	Lot #: Block #: Section #:
Description of the type of casket you would like:	
I would like the following Pall Bearers:	

Cremation:	○ Y ○ N
If you choose to be cremated, describe what you would like done with your ashes	

MEMORIAL

I would like flowers:	○ Y ○ N
If no, in lieu of flowers please make contributions to the following organizations:	

DONOR'S INFORMATION:
I [○ WISH] [○ DO NOT WISH] to make an anatomical gift, to take effect upon my death. If you do wish to make such a gift, we recommend you specify which body parts you are willing to donate and include a copy of that document in this section. Keep the original in a secure place. Instructions regarding anatomical gifts need to be readily available within hours of death.

SIGNATURE: _____

DATE: _____

(167)

Funeral Special Requests

Form 56

Updated:

Obituary Reading:

Tombstone Engraving:

Organs for Donation:

Other Special Requests:

I would like the following songs, music, scripture, poetry, etc. at my funeral:

Funeral Special Requests (continued)

FORM 57

Updated: _____

I currently have the following pets: _____

I ask that _____ take care of such pets for the rest of their lives.

In the event of my death, the following is additional information which I think is important for my family and advisors to know:

People to Notify:	
Name:	Name:
Relationship:	Relationship:
Phone:	Phone:
Cell:	Cell:
Name:	Name:
Relationship:	Relationship:
Phone:	Phone:
Cell:	Cell:
Name:	Name:
Relationship:	Relationship:
Phone:	Phone:
Cell:	Cell:
Name:	Name:
Relationship:	Relationship:
Phone:	Phone:
Cell:	Cell:

(171)

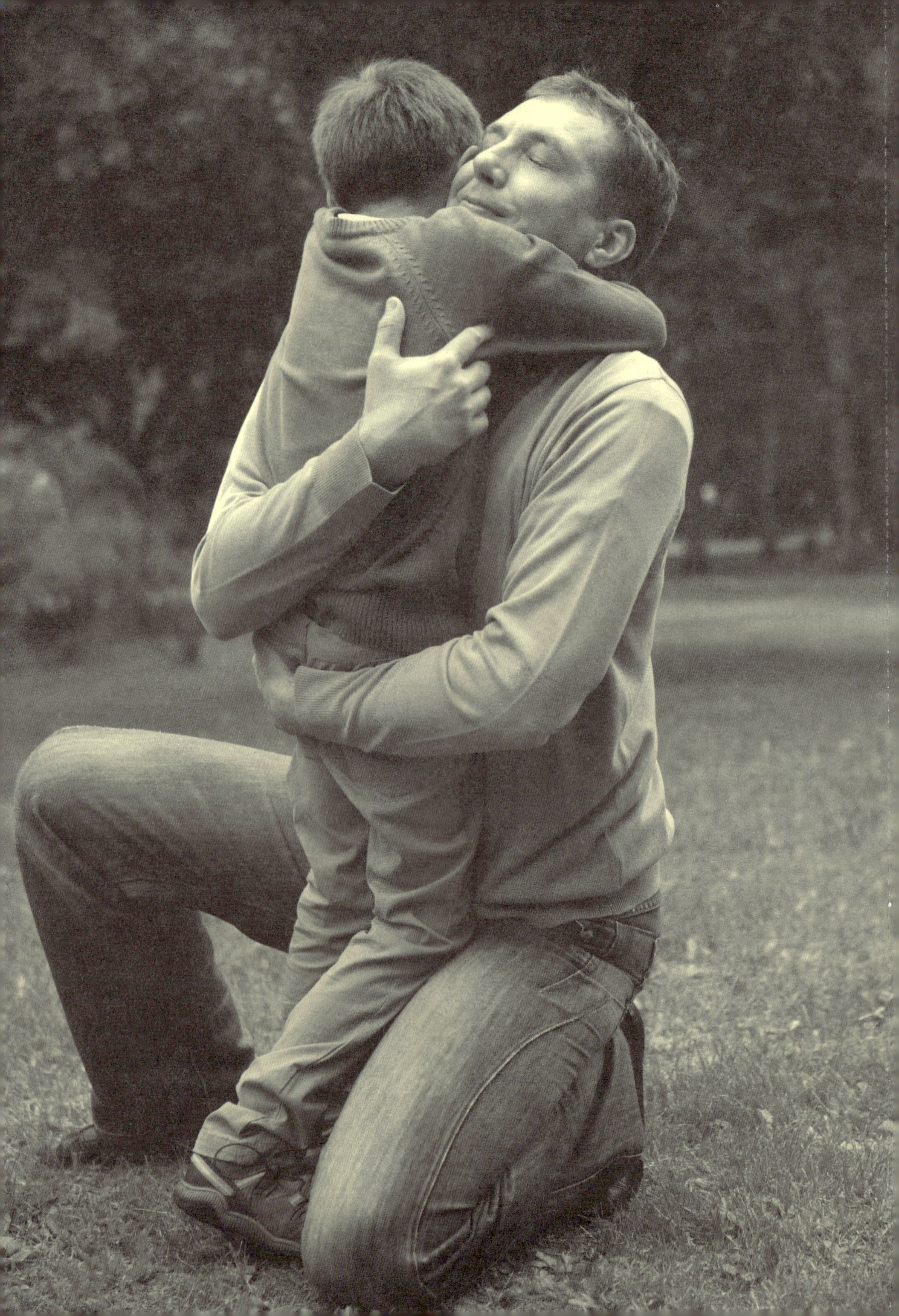

CHAPTER 7

From *Value* to *Hope*

GENERATIONAL THINKING

One of my favorite pictures is a black and white photograph that was taken when Eisenhower was President. It is a snapshot of my grandfather and me. He was sitting in his favorite chair. I was behind him playing peek-a-boo by moving back and forth to each side of the chair. My mother caught the Kodak moment and in it captured an expression that has left an incredible imprint. The look on my grandfather's face is priceless. I know that look. It's the same smiling eyes, the same comfortable grin, the same expression of joy and satisfaction that my countenance reflects when I am around my grandsons.

My grandfather loved me. I suspect that if he had written his thoughts, they would resonate with the generational feelings of fulfillment; the emotions, love and hope that I hold regarding Ryan Jr. and Rogan. Today everyone in our family speaks well of my grandfather. He died when I was in 4th grade. Everything I remember about him affirms the accolades given by my mother and my aunts and uncles. I would love to read his words, capture a deeper look into his heart, gain insight from his thoughts, learn more about his story, feel his struggles and be encouraged and motivated by his hope.

My grandfather was a man of faith. He loved God, acknowledged Jesus as his Savior and desired to serve Him well. What was his spiritual journey? What characteristics of God did he discover? What did he wrestle with? What did he learn that helped him most? If there was *one thing* that he could share about his relationship with God, what would it be? A document like this I would keep in a special place in my library. I would read it and share it with my children and grandchildren.

Forms 58 – 70

This final chapter of *Unfinished Business* is dedicated to helping all of us communicate and organize on paper words with generational value. Procrastination is an enemy that stands in the way of finishing the previous chapter because chapter six requires professional and legal input from others in order to complete all the files. Procrastination can also stand in the way of finishing this chapter because Chapter 7 requires quite a bit of thought and writing. You will need to carve out chunks of time. In addition to filling in forms on family history and personal history, you will be recalling important experiences, family memories, important traditions and key events. You will be commenting on character traits that you observe and lessons you have learned. You will be sharing thoughts and advice along with your values and hopes.

Writing is not easy, but don't let the thought of putting pen to paper slow you down. If you follow a few basic steps, you will find that most of these topics almost write themselves. With the right format, your main focus will be supplying ideas, which is the most important part. The following simple steps should help guide you through the writing process:

- Focus on the topic
- Picture the specific people for whom you are writing this memo
- Speak to them
- Prepare an outline of your ideas
- Write a thesis statement on what you hope to accomplish
- Write the body
    > First jot down the main points
    > Follow this with sub-points
    > Elaborate on the sub-points
- Write the introduction
- Write the conclusion
- Read it over and add the finishing touches

Organizing is a big part of the battle. So is enjoying the process. As you question the value of what you are doing, think of what this would mean to you if you were on the receiving end. Stay focused on the persons for whom you are writing this. Picture them sitting in front of you. If you are able to do that you will remain motivated and your words will come from the heart, not just the head.

There really isn't anything in these forms that is revolutionary. This book is designed to help men think, structure, organize and complete things that may otherwise remain unfinished business.

Moses documented his story and communicated a perspective on this life that provides depth, meaning and balance for what we see today and what lays ahead. Take a look at Deuteronomy chapter 6 as further example of Moses' writings and communication. Joseph provides a living example of firmly establishing priority around future hope and then managing personal affairs, right down to the instructions concerning his bones, to align with that hope.

Earlier this year, I received a call from my parents. I was in Colorado having dinner at the home of one of our store owners. I let the first call roll into voice mail, but when they called back a short time later, I suspected some urgency and excused myself from the table. My parents never call my cell phone back to back. I stepped outside and was immediately relieved when I heard the excitement in my mother's voice. They had spent most of that day with an old friend of mine. Tim and I graduated from high school together. Today he owns several funeral homes around the Milwaukee area. My parents had decided that they wanted to put the affairs surrounding their death in order so they called Tim.

As I stood on the back deck overlooking Colorado Springs, my mother and father explained with enthusiasm the decisions they had made. They shared that they had talked with my brothers and sisters earlier and everyone was relieved to know that all of this was addressed. As they described some of the details of their decisions I thought to myself, this is a moment I will probably never forget. My parents sounded as excited about their funerals as planning our family Christmas gathering, summer picnic reunion or their upcoming 60th wedding anniversary. The excitement I sensed came not from the events that will surround their funeral, but from the satisfaction that their affairs were in order. They finished a piece of business that most leave unfinished.

As you finish Chapter 7, I hope you have that same feeling of excitement and fulfillment. You are completing a worthy work. We were hardwired by God to be relational. He built us to know Him and to be known by Him. As a natural extension, we desire to know and to be known by others. Stories play an important role in this. There is power and life-application in our stories. Stories too often go untold. Personal experiences, lessons, beliefs, values and hope should be shared with our family and friends. Take your time and tell your stories well.

Congratulations to you for taking the initiative to put your affairs in order. Finishing the seven chapters in *Unfinished Business* has required perspective, discipline and effort. Remember that the work is not done. Continue to update appropriate information on an annual basis.

When your life here ends, when all the pieces of the "game" we have played on earth "go back in the box," when it is only you and God, when perspective forever changes, I pray your life will have glorified Him and you will realize the complete fulfillment of your hope.

May this work which you are completing always be relationally centered, which is how we were created. May this work reflect a well-placed hope that finds its home in God's presence.

Family History

FORM 58

Updated: _____

I was born in _____ on _____.
                 City, State   *Month, Day Year*

My parents are/were _____ and _____.
                   Full Name   *Full Name*

My maternal grandparents are/were _____ and _____.
                               Full Name   *Full Name*

My paternal grandparents are/were _____ and _____.
                               Full Name   *Full Name*

I have the following brothers and sisters (including step and half-siblings):

_____ Born _____

_____ Born _____

_____ Born _____

_____ Born _____

_____ Born _____

My children are: ○ I have no children.

_____ Born _____

_____ Born _____

_____ Born _____

_____ Born _____

_____ Born _____

I was adopted and my birth mother and father are/were: _____

I [○ HAVE] [○ DO NOT HAVE] detailed information on my family's history. It is located at:

_____

_____

Some important facts about my family history:

_____

_____

_____

_____

Personal Values

FORM 59

Updated: _____

Some of my fondest memories include:

_____
_____
_____
_____

Some of my hardest times and biggest struggles include:

_____
_____
_____
_____

I believe that the most important things in life are:

_____
_____
_____
_____

The most significant things I have done in my life are:

_____
_____
_____
_____

Some of the most significant things I have learned from my experiences are:

_____
_____
_____
_____

Personal Values (continued)

FORM 60

Updated: _____

It is my hope that my family will use its inheritance from me to help accomplish the following goals in their lives:

_____
_____
_____
_____

My values can be summed up as follows:

_____
_____
_____
_____

My hope can be summed up as follows:

_____
_____
_____
_____

How I would like to be remembered:

_____
_____
_____
_____
_____

Attached are my favorite: ○ Poem(s)   ○ Quote(s)   ○ Scripture(s)   ○ Story(s)   ○ Verse(s)

Personal History

FORM 61

Updated: _____

Full Name:	SSN:
Marital Status: ○ Married ○ Single ○ Widowed ○ Divorced	
Street Address:	Phone:
City, State, Zip:	
Date of Birth:	Birthplace:
Birth Certificate Location:	
US citizen? ○ Y ○ N If no, describe:	

SPOUSE

Name:	SSN:
Date of Birth:	Birthplace:
US citizen? ○ Y ○ N If no, describe:	

PARENTS

Father's Name:	
Date of Birth:	Birthplace:
Mother's Name:	
Date of Birth:	Birthplace:

EDUCATION

College:	Degree:
Address:	Date:

INVOLVEMENTS

MILITARY SERVICE

Branch:	Enlist Date:
Rank Achieved:	Discharge Date:
Honors:	

(183)

Personal History (continued)

FORM 62

Updated: _____

SERVICE AND SOCIAL INVOLVEMENTS

SPECIAL RECOGNITIONS

CHURCH

Name:		Phone:	
Address:			
City, State, Zip:			

CAREER

Name:		Phone:	
Address:			
City, State, Zip:			

POSITION AND ACHIEVEMENTS

Spouse / Children Family Tree
(Update annually)

FORM 63

Updated: _____

Name:		Birthdate:	

Memories:

Spouse:		Birthdate:	

Memories:

Child:		Birthdate:	

Memories:

Child:		Birthdate:	

Memories:

Child:		Birthdate:	

Memories:

Grandchild:		Birthdate:	

Memories:

Grandchild:		Birthdate:	

Memories:

Parents / Grandparents / Great Grandparents Family Tree

FORM 64

Name:		Birthdate:	
Traditions (Involvements & Achievements)		Relation:	

Name:		Birthdate:	
Traditions (Involvements & Achievements)		Relation:	

Name:		Birthdate:	
Traditions (Involvements & Achievements)		Relation:	

Name:		Birthdate:	
Traditions (Involvements & Achievements)		Relation:	

Name:		Birthdate:	
Traditions (Involvements & Achievements)		Relation:	

Name:		Birthdate:	
Traditions (Involvements & Achievements)		Relation:	

Name:		Birthdate:	
Traditions (Involvements & Achievements)		Relation:	

Family Tree Resources

Creating your first family tree is fast and easy. If you would like to establish a family tree go to one of many helpful websites: HTTP://WWW.FAMILYTREE.COM

Searches related to Family Tree and much more:

- How to make a family tree
- Create family tree
- Print family tree
- Family tree templates
- Family tree examples
- Blank family tree
- People Search

What About Re-Marriage?

If you would like your marriage partner to have the freedom and to re-marry then it would be a good idea to include a letter stating such to help remove any guilt or sense of obligation.

If you would like to protect the inheritance that you leave to existing family members without the danger of it being deluded or spread into future family additions, a statement to that regard should be included. A professional attorney or accountant would be able to help set up the proper legal structure to protect all assets including protection should any future marriage end in divorce.

When Your Marital Status Changes

FORM 67

Updated: _____

Marital status may change because of marriage, divorce or death. Regardless of the cause, you will need to notify some people and make some changes. This checklist has been designed as a guide during this time of transition.

CHECKLIST:

- ❍ Revise or have will drawn by an attorney.
- ❍ Change beneficiaries on life insurance policies.
- ❍ Change beneficiaries on pension or retirement plans.
- ❍ Change beneficiaries on stocks and bonds.
- ❍ Change name of insured on homeowner's or fire insurance policy.
- ❍ Change name of insured on car insurance policy.
- ❍ Change or cancel credit cards.
- ❍ Change name on checking, savings and investment accounts.
- ❍ Notify your company's payroll department of changes in names and address, as well as tax exemption changes.
- ❍ Report name and any address changes to the Motor Vehicle Department, so that car registration(s) and operator's license(s) may be updated.
- ❍ File address change with the Post Office.
- ❍ Set a date to pay your bills each month, so that no interest or late charges will have to be paid.
- ❍ Change name on real estate deeds.

When Your Marital Status Changes

Updated: _____

Marital status may change because of marriage, divorce or death. Regardless of the cause, you will need to notify some people and make some changes. This checklist has been designed as a guide during this time of transition.

Checklist:

- ○ Revise or have will drawn by an attorney.
- ○ Change beneficiaries on life insurance policies.
- ○ Change beneficiaries on pension or retirement plans.
- ○ Change beneficiaries on stocks and bonds.
- ○ Change name of insured on homeowner's or fire insurance policy.
- ○ Change name of insured on car insurance policy.
- ○ Change or cancel credit cards.
- ○ Change name on checking, savings and investment accounts.
- ○ Notify your company's payroll department of changes in names and address, as well as tax exemption changes.
- ○ Report name and any address changes to the Motor Vehicle Department, so that car registration(s) and operator's license(s) may be updated.
- ○ File address change with the Post Office.
- ○ Set a date to pay your bills each month, so that no interest or late charges will have to be paid.
- ○ Change name on real estate deeds.

Individual Letters

Take the appropriate time to personalize individual letters sharing thoughts and advice with each of those closest to you. These lasting thoughts and words of advise should come from your heart, your experience and your best desires.

Following are some of the topics you may consider including;

- Characteristics and strengths you observe in that person

- Encouragement to be themselves, to celebrate who they are, and to exercise their gifts

- Favorite memories you have involving that person

- Life Lesson(s) you have learned

- Something about their character

- Truth(s) from God's Word

- Your prayer for that person

- Your blessings on that person

Memo to My Family

FORM 69

While the individual letters should have covered specific things relating directly to each person, this memo to your family will serve as an overall final message of your temporal desires and, more importantly, your eternal hope.

Included should be:

- Your conversion story / testimony

- Your life verse(s)

- What you have learned regarding the attributes of God and His character

- Your encouragement regarding life focus, walking with God and what it means to bring glory to Him

- Final words of appreciation and perspective

- A summary of your hope

Closing Summary

FORM 70

Updated: _____

To: _____

This book has been prepared to aid my loved ones following my death. I also plan to refer to this book concerning important matters during my lifetime.

Revision will be a continuous need, and I have planned to review it frequently.

Most people desire that their financial house be set in order. I have completed this notebook as a token of love for my family. It will also help assisting survivors in the settlement of estate matters at my death. Most importantly it will help serve to bring focus and attention to my eternal hope through our Lord Jesus Christ.

SIGNATURE: _____

DATE: _____

Warning

Identity theft has become a major problem in the United States. *Unfinished Business* is purposely designed to provide your family and advisors with as much information as possible about you and your personal financials. It is also information, which in the wrong hands, could help someone steal your identity and/or your assets. We strongly advise you to (1) keep all document copies in a locked location which is only accessible by people you fully trust and (2) provide copies of *Unfinished Business* documents only to persons who you are confident can be trusted to maintain the secrecy of your information.

(204)